BASIC AND ADVANCED
LIGHT PLANE MAINTENANCE

Firewall Forward
—Top End

The Light Plane Maintenance Library
Volume One

BASIC AND ADVANCED
LIGHT PLANE MAINTENANCE

Firewall Forward
—Top End

By the Editors of *Light Plane*
Maintenance Magazine

Belvoir Publications, Inc.
Riverside, Connecticut

ISBN: 0-9615196-2-2

Please Note: The information appearing in this publication is presented for educational purposes only. In no case shall the publishers be held responsible for any use readers may choose to make (or not to make) of this information. Readers are hereby advised that Federal Aviation Regulation 91.163(a) places primary responsibility for ensuring the airworthy condition of any aircraft on the aircraft owner or operator. Any person who performs inspections, alterations, and/or repairs on any aircraft does so entirely at his or her own risk.

Contents

Preface

This is the first in a series of guides comprising The Light Plane Maintenance Library and dedicated to informing airplane owners and pilots about means of obtaining improved economy and performance from their aircraft. Their purpose is to describe preventive maintenance techniques in areas ranging from aircraft hardware and cost-saving inspection procedures to maintenance of the powerplant, airframe, interior, electronics, undercarriage and other items.

These books are derived from materials that have appeared over several years in *Light Plane Maintenance Magazine,* the most highly respected general aviation journal of its kind. In these pages, the staff of *LPM* offers its expertise based on years of close, often professional, familiarity with regulations, methods, opportunities and pitfalls in a form organized to help the reader save expense and difficulty while enhancing his flying safety.

One of the most glaring and costly inadequacies in pilot education today is the failure to ensure that pilots will understand the equipment they fly. When an engine coughs, a strut goes flat, a radio dies, or other problems occur, the average pilot reflexively turns to a professional mechanic to right the wrong. In many cases that's proper, for the FARs reserve to certified mechanics the bulk of major maintenance work—but by no means all the maintenance that might be performed. There still is left to the owner a significant amount of preventive maintenance, on his own authority or under a certified mechanic's supervision. It can be very expensive for an owner not to take advantage of savings in labor costs, not to mention his or her right to purchase parts at discount prices.

It can be even more expensive—*and dangerous*—when pilots fail to *detect* that something is wrong with their aircraft until a catastrophic failure occurs. Many pilots believe they preflight and monitor their aircraft thoroughly and efficiently, but they all too often don't know what to watch, listen, and feel for before, during and after flight.

We trust our lives to the devices we fly, yet more than we would like to admit, we trust not on the basis of knowledgeable familiarity but of blind faith. Therefore, for a pilot to delve into the innards of his airplane—if only to learn through reading how the systems work—is

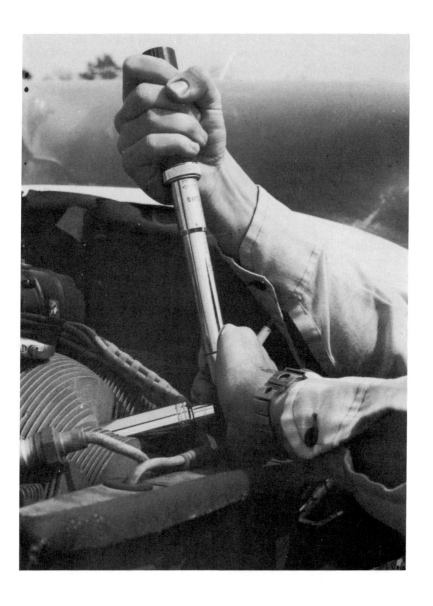

to add a vital measure of safety to each flight. This book and its companion volumes are designed to make that familiarity possible, just as they are meant to make legal owner-performed maintenance feasible, rewarding, and safe.

You will find a strong personal element in these pages. The *LPM* staff takes preventive maintenance and what it means very much to heart. These discussions are based on hands-on experience, and as a result, some of the procedural descriptions take the form of actual case histories. As many an aspiring mechanic has found, learning often can best be encouraged by looking over a working expert's shoulder. When we describe a technique in this manner, we do so in confidence that the example will be applicable not only to the type aircraft at hand but most likely to types our readers will be working on. The articles on which this book is based were written with the reader's interests foremost in mind, and that spirit has been sustained in the preparation of this book.

We have tried to maintain clarity in organizing a highly complex body of material. Inevitably and intentionally, some repetition of certain points will occur. We believe that in trying to follow complex technical material, the reader will appreciate the ease of continuity such repetition can provide.

In the appendices to this volume, we offer engine troubleshooting guides. Similar guides will appear in further volumes. We recommend keeping these guides handy for reference as we discuss various engine problems from book to book.

Finally, the danger of error through obsolescence has discouraged us (except where specifically noted) from quoting prices and costs and referring to individual firms and shops. For current information on costs and services, we recommend that the reader consult *Light Plane Maintenance Magazine*.

Riverside, Connecticut
March 1987

Part I
CYLINDERS

Chapter 1

THE TOP OVERHAUL

For many aircraft owners, putting their machines in the hands of shops for potentially major-cost work is only slightly less daunting than heading for the hospital for an amputation of the cranium. Two such jobs are annual inspections and major overhauls, but the piece of work over which owners are most likely to lose their heads is the top overhaul, during which the most severely tested portion of the engine receives close scrutiny and, perhaps, some help.

When the cylinders are involved, it follows that in that searing locale, wear and tear, the scars of time and violence, come with the territory. Along with them come cost, inconvenience and hard questions. For attention must be paid to these scars, and questions must be answered as to when to apply remedies and how many remedies to apply in order to protect your engine without wiping out your bank account.

In this chapter, we will look at top overhauls in general. In the following chapters, we will examine the engine area and parts that the top overhaul usually concerns.

WHEN IS IT NECESSARY?

The "top overhaul" is to aircraft maintenance what the coronary bypass is to medicine: a costly, controversial procedure designed to prolong life or forestall the inevitable, depending on your point of view. The cost is high, the outcome uncertain. To be sure, the top overhaul (or "ring and valve job," in automotive parlance) has its place in aircraft maintenance. But it's also one of the most oversold procedures in aviation. Got a low jug? "Let's top it, " the mechanic says. On inspection, the cylinder is beyond limits. Want to grind it oversize? Okay. "But if we grind *one* jug oversize, you really should do the others, too." (Another famous sales pitch: "You know, there really isn't that much additional labor to do all four cylinders, as opposed to just one ...")

A statement once made by Joe Diblin (when he was Lycoming's chief of customer relations) underscores this point. "It's unfortunate,"

Diblin remarked, "that too many people are spending money need-lessly on top overhaul." It was—and still is— Lycoming's contention that with proper care, and "fairly frequent flight" (defined by Lycoming as 15 hours per month), most engines should reach their normal TBO without a top overhaul along the way.

Some operators do top overhauls prematurely, and there's little doubt that many of these are a waste of money. But some operators are utilizing the top overhaul as part of a carefully considered game plan for extending TBO (time between major overhauls). The market for the "TBO-extension" top overhaul, in fact, seems to be growing rapidly. Many questions *LPM* gets run along the lines of: "Should I major the engine at the factory-recommended TBO, or should I top it now and try for TBO-plus-400?" And: "If I top it, when should I top it?" "What should a decent top consist of ?" "Who should do the work?" "How should the engine be broken in?"

These are not easy questions. They're a lot harder when you're cheek-to-jowl with Mr. Goodwrench. Then, it's best to have the answers in advance.

Definition of Terms

The term "top overhaul" means many different things to many different people. In some quarters it means pulling the cylinders off, inspecting them, repairing them as needed, and putting them right back in service with as few new parts as possible. To some, it means a complete ring and valve job, to new limits, for every cylinder. To still others, it means reworking just the jugs that need to be reworked. (Everybody agrees on one thing, which is that the word "top" in "top overhaul" refers to the cylinders and reciprocating parts of an engine, as opposed to the "bottom end," which consists of the crankshaft, camshaft, crankcase, main bearings, oil sump, and gear train.)

Broadly speaking, then, a "top overhaul" can be considered any operation that results in the removal of one or more cylinders and the refurbishment (if not the actual replacement) of worn top-end components. As such, it has its counterpart in the turbine "hot section" inspection, which for most jet engines is a required event each 1,200 hours or so. Turbine engines are enormously expensive to overhaul— $60,000 for even the smallest Garrett—and to have to tear one down every 2,000 hours would be unthinkable; since most of the wear and tear occurs in the hot parts of the engine, it only stands to reason that the "hot section" should be inspected between major overhauls, and

The "top end" of a piston engine—that is, the cylinders and everything inside them and reciprocating parts of the engine. The top end is analogous to the "hot section" of a turbojet. Few jet engines reach TBO without a hot section overhaul along the way, and the same can be said for many large piston powerplants.

the TBO extended to some fairly high value based on the results of previous hot-section inspections.

The same line of reasoning can be applied to piston engines. The highest temperatures (and the most wear) occur in a piston engine's "top end": the cylinder barrels, pistons, rings, valves, guides, rocker bushings, etc. By inspecting and/or refurbishing the piston engine's "hot section" at regular intervals, it ought to be possible to raise the average piston engine's TBO. With the exception of the camshaft and accessory gearing, there is not much on the "bottom end" of the typical O-360 or O-470 (or O-520, etc.) that bears looking at much oftener than 2,400 hours, especially if the engine in question is being flown daily.

Many operators have used this approach to score big TBO gains, among them a California-based Cessna 421 operator whose Continental GTSIO-520-D engines—nominal TBO: 1,200 hours—went all the way to 2,350 hours before being majored, thanks to scrupulous top-end renewal at 650 and 1,350 hours (and good operator technique, of course). A Part 135 operator obtained FAA approval for 3,000-hour

TBOs on Continental IO-520s based on mandatory top overhauls at 1,500 hours. (FAA-sanctioned TBO extensions of 200 to 300 hours for air-taxi operators are extremely common, even without mandatory top overhauls.)

Overall Economics

The economics of performing a top (or partial top—i.e., a top-overhaul of two or three cylinders) as a preliminary to TBO-busting are worth pondering carefully, particularly if the engine in question is already nearing TBO. There's a rule of thumb for this, fortunately. Consider what has to happen in order for a $4,000 top overhaul to be cost-effective in the case of an engine that is nearing TBO and costs $8,000 to major. Obviously, for the top overhaul to be worthwhile, a TBO extension of 50 percent (4,000 divided by 8,000) must be achieved—e.g., your O-320 would have to go to 3,000 hours (vs. the factory TBO of 2,000), and at that point, you would simply have broken even on the top overhaul. (It will have just paid for itself in terms of forestalling the major.)

But let's look at the case of the Turbo Saratoga owner who—when the time comes—is planning not to overhaul but to buy a factory zero-time rebuilt Lycoming TIO-540-S1AD at a cost of $23,000. In this instance, a top overhaul billing out at $4,000 will be cost-effective if a mere 17-percent TBO extension can be achieved. Since the factory TBO is 1,800 hours, this puts the break-even point at 2,106 hours—by no means an impossible goal.

One conclusion is clear. If your engine has a low TBO or is expensive to major (or you intend to spend a great deal of money on a replacement engine from the factory), a late-in-the-TBO-cycle top overhaul is more apt to be cost-effective than if your engine is a cheap one to overhaul and carries a high TBO.

Lycoming top-end parts are more expensive, generally, than Continental parts (Lycoming's sodium-filled exhaust valves, in particular, cost double or triple what most Continental valves do), and Lycoming engines tend to have generous TBOs, which might suggest that a top overhaul (for TBO-extension purposes) would more often be cost-effective for Continental owners than for Lycoming owners. This may be true to some extent, but labor is usually a bigger factor, overall, than parts in the top overhaul bottom line. So essentially the same rules apply to Lycoming as to Continental owners.

With turbocharged engines, additional considerations apply. Will overhaul time. One or more of these accessories will likely need replacing somewhere down the TBO line, if not at the time of the top overhaul. Performing a top overhaul doesn't allow you to defer *all* decision-making with regard to life-limited components.

Prophylaxis versus Repair

There may be special circumstances under which a top overhaul performed pre-emptively (prophylactically) is warranted—for example, if you are running a Part 135 operation and have a TBO waiver from the FAA requiring you to top your engines every 1,000 hours—but generally speaking, for most operators, top overhauls should not be done on a time schedule. They should be done when top-end components are in definite need of inspection and/or repair, as evidenced by the presence of clear-cut distress symptoms.

By a "clear-cut symptom," we don't mean cylinder compression in the sixties. In our opinion, far too many owners are being bamboozled into taking cylinders off simply on the basis of "poor compression," which most mechanics erroneously define as 60/80.

Some time ago, Joe Diblin commented in the Avco Lycoming *Flyer:* "It has been our experience that either method of compression investigation [direct, or differential] can be handled in such a way as to give almost any reading. This does not [mean] that there are necessarily dishonest mechanics, but it is an attempt to advise operators that *cylinders should not be pulled indiscriminately, based on a single set of readings."*

There is no FAA rule requiring cylinders to be removed when differential compression goes below 60/80. (If your A&P disagrees with this statement, ask him to produce the regulation.) FAA Advisory Circular 43.13-1A does contain guidelines for compression testing, but AC 43.13-1A is *advisory only* and does not carry the force of law. Likewise, manufacturers' bulletins are *advisory,* not mandatory, except that they may require the use of special tools per Federal Aviation Regulation 43.13, paragraph (a). On compression scores, the regulations are silent. And rightfully so.

Space won't permit us to recount the litany of compression-score myths here. (We still shake our heads, though, when we read the line about "compression 75 percent of new" in the Price Digest Bluebook description of "average" plane condition. Compression in a new engine is never 80/80, and seldom 78/80. Therefore "75 percent of new" implies something below 60/80.) The important thing to remember is that most "20/80" and "30/80" cylinders fly in to the shop where they're eventually removed, so low compression is not really a safety-of-flight concern. Certainly, 60/80 doesn't qualify as dangerously low compression.

How low is low? Some years ago, Teledyne Continental issued a bulletin to Tiara engine operators (M76-18, Rev. 1) stating that compressions as low as 60/80 "are common readings for new engines," and a "limit reading of down to 55/80 is permissible."

The Pasadena, California, Police Department operates a small fleet of Enstrom F-28C helicopters powered by Lycoming HIO-360-E1AD engines (with Rajay turbos); and PPD's resident IA-A&P doesn't begin to consider a low jug a problem until it goes below 55/80. If a cylinder is between 55/80 and 60/80, it will be continued in service and monitored every five to ten hours.

We agree with these guidelines. Even if a jug shows up 40/80, it should not be pulled indiscriminately (unless the engine shows other signs of distress). Before pulling a jug on compression alone, its valves should be staked (see AC 43.13-1A) and the rings oiled, and compression measured a second and third time, using a different test rig, before condemning the cylinder as defective.

High oil consumption (one quart per hour) *might* be a good reason to top an engine—if other distress signs are evident (e.g., poor power output, wet spark plugs, low compression). But even oil wetness on top-hole spark plugs—a classic indication of advanced barrel and/or ring wear—doesn't *necessarily* mean you're looking at a top overhaul for the associated jug(s). In a fuel-injected engine, wet plugs (possibly accompanied by degraded performance and a rise in oil usage) can simply mean clogged injector nozzles. "A typical complaint from the field," one Lycoming official notes, "will be reported to us at the factory as a loss of power and the cylinders pumping oil. It is typically caused by a dirty or restricted fuel nozzle. The oil residue is a result of insufficient fuel causing low combustion pressures, which prevent the piston rings from doing their job efficiently. Without proper combustion pressures, we do not have sufficient pressure on the compression ring, which allows the oil to leak past."

The main thing to remember is that when deciding on the need for a top overhaul, trouble symptoms—not Hobbs time—should be your main concern; and no *one* indication of cylinder health should be relied on totally for making the "top" decision (unless, of course, there's a gaping hole in the side of a cylinder). Look at the total picture. Cross-

Once you are committed to a top overhaul, insist on thoroughness. The cylinders should be cleaned up prior to being checked for choke and bore discrepancies as well as for step-wear and out-of-round. A thorough top will also include a dye-penetrant inspection for cracks.

compare different indicators—compression, oil analysis, spark plug deposits, engine vibration, oil consumption, etc.—and *monitor trends;* don't fixate on individual data points. If damage to piston crowns, valves, valve seats, cylinder heads, or cylinder walls is suspected, remember that these areas can be checked without removing the cylinder(s), through borescoping. (Also, valve-to-guide clearances can be monitored from the rocker box end using the techniques described in Lycoming Service Instruction S.I. 1088). In short, don't pull a jug unless the handwriting on the cylinder wall is both legible and inescapable.

THE WELL-TEMPERED TOP

That handwriting's tipping of the scales won't relieve you of further decisions that could either save you what could have been heavier future expenses or burden you more than a sensible top overhaul should. Choosing wisely means balancing and mixing the elements of effectiveness and economy realistically.

Cutting Corners

Once the decision has been made to pull a cylinder, don't scrimp or cut corners. Have the jug checked out thoroughly, especially if it's an oldie (more than 1,800 hours TT). If your A&P isn't equipped to perform detailed cleaning, inspection, and repair work on cylinders, have your errant jug(s) shipped to a properly qualified FAA Repair Station (ECI, Schneck, Van Dusen, Piedmont). That way, if special repairs are needed, they can be made on-site in minimum time. Don't expect your local mechanic to be able to weld head cracks or grind barrels oversize.

Avoid doing a "quick-and-dirty" ring job in the field to correct low compression or high oil consumption. If a preliminary dimensional check of your cylinders for bore, out-of-round, step-wear, choke, etc. shows the jug(s) to be within service limits, but not within new limits, stop and ask yourself a few hard questions. What is your goal for the top overhaul? If it's merely to improve compression, you may be justified in fitting new rings to the cylinder, honing it, and putting it back in service essentially unchanged. Likewise, if all that's wrong with your jugs is glazed barrels, go ahead and hone them to break the glaze, then put them back in service (with new rings, if more than 50 hours old). If on the other hand you're trying to eliminate oil consumption in a large Continental, or continue an engine past TBO (to the point where the top overhaul will pay for itself), you should definitely bring the cylinder back to new limits. That will usually mean an oversize grind or chroming the barrel; replacing the exhaust valve guide (and the valve, if it's deformed); fitting all-new rings; and possibly replacing the piston itself, if lands are worn or sideplay in the barrel has grown.

If the exhaust valve-to-guide side play is at all sloppy (consult your Table of Limits), don't expect the jug to make TBO-plus without replacing the guide. Take this opportunity to upgrade to the latest applicable guide and valve P/Ns. (Consult the latest revision of Lycoming Service Instruction No. 1037 or Continental M82-6, as applicable.) But be sure your shop *hones the guides* to proper finish before putting valves in them. Lycoming S.I. No. 1200C specifies a 30-microinch (RMS) surface crosshatch on the guide I.D. (internal diameter) for best service life. Many A&Ps aren't even aware of this.

Cylinder honing is another gray area for many mechanics. "Honing is critical for break-in," a Continental engineer told us. "And not many

Early in the top overhaul—after four to six hours of "removal" labor— you will be able to peer inside the cylinders to survey the damage, an education in itself.

mechanics know how to do it right. The scratches in the barrel bore should be crossed, with lines running at an angle of 22 to 32 degrees with the end of the barrel. These scratches must be wet-cut uniformly in both directions. The final pattern must be clean cut, not sharp, and totally free of torn or folded metal. All of this is spelled out in Service Bulletin M73-13, Revision 1." Also spelled out in that bulletin is a requirement for the final hone to finish out at 15 to 30 micro-inches (except at the extreme ends of the barrel, where 45 micro-inches is acceptable).

According to Continental, it is okay to run figure-eights around the barrel I.D. with 200-grit sandpaper after honing to ensure removal of ridges and torn metal.

Very important: If the cylinder is to be oven-heated for valve guide replacement (or other repair operations), be sure honing is done *after*—never before—oven treatment, since otherwise residues from the kerosene-type oils used in the honing process will cook down to form varnish during the heating up of the barrel(s), thereby glazing the cylinders and preventing proper break-in.

This Continental jug has been ground .015-over, which is indicated on its hold-down flange. While Lycomings can be ground .010- or .020-inch oversize (they are color keyed to indicate which), Continentals are limited to .015 (and are always stamped).

Chrome Versus Oversize

Suppose your barrels are scored (from too many cold starts without a preheat). Or your rings have stuck (or have begun to stick), creating a nasty wear step on the barrel I.D. at the top of ring travel. Or suppose your jugs are okay for I.D. and out-of-round, but can't be cleaned up while also maintaining the proper choke contour. (That is, if you regrind to restore taper, you no longer meet service limits for bore diameter.) The latter is not an uncommon problem in certain large Continentals. "If you take a cylinder off a Pressurized Centurion after 800 hours," one engine man told us flatly, "you can be damn sure the choke will be gone, and the cylinder can't be returned to service."

The next step is usually to grind oversize, or chrome the barrel. Which should you do?

The answer is easy if you own a late-model Lycoming. All current production Lycoming engines except O-235-C, O-320-A/C/E, and IO-320-A or C employ nitrided (surface hardened) barrels. And nitrided barrels *cannot* be ground oversize, except for O-360-B and D and O-540-B barrels, which can be ground .010-inch over. (For more information, refer to Lycoming Service Instruction No. 1047 and the *Direct Drive Overhaul Manual*.)

Barring the above caveat, Lycoming operators with standard steel jugs actually enjoy a somewhat greater flexibility than Continental owners when it comes to oversize grinding, since standard-steel Lycoming barrels can be ground .010-inch oversize *or* .020-inch oversize (Lycoming supplies rings and pistons in both oversizes), whereas Continental jugs can be ground .015-over only. If you see green paint on a Lycoming jug, it means the jug is .010-over. Yellow paint at the base of the cylinder signifies .020-over. Orange paint in the hold-down area means the cylinder has been chromed. (Continental jugs that have been ground .015-over are not color-keyed but have ".015" impression-stamped into the cylinder hold-down flange—and written in the logbooks.)

The decision whether to chrome or go oversize is often a tough one; many factors must be considered. Are rings readily available? Chrome cylinders require special rings—namely, non-chromed, cast-iron rings—and supply problems are not uncommon. (For example, until recently there were no aftermarket suppliers of chrome-cylinder ring sets for O-235 Lycomings, and the Lycoming factory's inventory of these rings was low, leaving some customers grounded for an entire season while overhaulers waited for rings to become available.) Oversize rings are also occasionally hard to get for certain engines. Ditto for oversize pistons, which are not sold in great volume and therefore are priced higher than the corresponding normal-size pistons.

New pistons are required when an oversize grind is done, whereas when cylinders are chromed back to normal (new) dimensions, old pistons can be reused. But it is often the case that pistons must be replaced anyway, due to normal wear. (Piston replacement is not a bad idea, also, if TBO-busting is being contemplated.) The picture is further clouded by the fact that most shops will tell you that if one jug is ground oversize, its opposite mate should be ground over as well, to maintain dynamic balance. (The Avco Lycoming *Direct Drive Overhaul Manual* recommends oversizing cylinders and pistons in pairs for this reason.) So while the chroming operation usually costs a minimum of $175 per cylinder, versus only $50 or so to grind a jug oversize, the price disparity between the two operations is mooted by considerations involving pistons, rings, and further work on other cylinders. If only one jug is bad, the most cost-effective solution may just be to replace the cylinder assembly with a new one.

Do all cylinders have to be chromed at once? No. There is no reason why chromed cylinders can't be mixed with steel cylinders on the same engine. ("It's done all the time," a spokesman for a major east-coast overhaul shop told us.) The important thing is not to mix chrome rings with non-chrome rings.

As for oversize grinding: We disagree with those who maintain that cylinders *must* be ground oversize in pairs, to maintain balance. Dynamic balance has less to do with the mass difference between oversize and standard pistons than it has to do with the combustion forces acting on opposite sides of the crank. (Uneven compression will cause worse vibration than unbalanced pistons.) Proof of the pudding is that when oversize and standard cylinders are mixed on the same engine, no difference is discernible in the cockpit.

Note: If a cylinder is cracked and it is repaired by welding, you will very likely end up having to regrind the barrel. The reason is that the heat of welding almost always causes some permanent distortion of the barrel, necessitating regrinding and chrome-plating to bring the bore back to standard dimensions.

In general, we're in favor of doing the least work possible, even if it means mixing chrome, standard, and/or oversize jugs on the same engine. There is no benefit to be gained from pulling jugs that don't need to be pulled. Of course, if cost is no object, go ahead and put your A&P's kids through college. But if cost is no object, you're in the minority.

Break-in Considerations

If we were forced to take sides in the chrome-vs.-oversize debate, at least where top overhauls are concerned, we'd probably choose oversize grinding as our initial preference. The reason is that steel cylinders (properly honed) give more predictable break-in than chromed jugs, on the whole. Because of its inherent hardness, chrome is a more difficult surface to "seat in to" for rings, and unless ring seating is done in a test cell, break-in is a hit-or-miss affair—definitley best left to the overhauling agency, if at all possible. (Also, cylinder chroming is still something of an art, and if not done well, oil control is poor. When chroming is being considered we recommend sticking with an established firm such as Engine Components Inc. or Schneck.) If you own a GTSIO-520, chroming is no longer recommended by the factory; see Continental Service Bulletin M85-8, dated July 3, 1985.

If your overhauler will guarantee break-in of chromed cylinders, fine. Properly broken in, chromed cylinders will last a good deal longer than steel cylinders (because of chrome's hardness); and for operators who fly infrequently or are based near the coast, chrome offers vastly reduced corrosion potential. Most overhaulers, however, will not guarantee break-in on their chromed cylinders unless the engine is removed from the airplane and run in a test stand. The "in-the-airplane" break-in record of chromed jugs is not particularly good.

With steel cylinders (standard or oversize), it is important to begin the break-in as soon as possible after the cylinders are mounted on the engine, since polished (or honed) steel surfaces very quickly turn to rust unless inhibited with corrosion-preventive oil. During the break-in process, the microscopic hills and valleys in the honed barrel metal fill with varnish and combustion products to form—in effect—a protective coating which helps slow the rapid corrosion that otherwise affects new cylinders. It's essential to start this process as soon as the plane leaves the shop.

More about break-in techniques shortly.

Little Known Facts and Common Mistakes

If you are assisting in the performance of your top overhaul—or merely watching the process with an eye for saving money—you'll want to watch out for common (and potentially expensive) *faux pas* and be aware of some important facts.

• A common mistake in field overhauls is to install piston rings upside-down. Even if a ring looks symmetrical, it should be installed with the part-number side *up*, facing the top of the piston.

• Polished steel parts should not be touched with bare hands. Skin salts and acids can corrode bare steel in a very short time. Bare steel parts should be coated with oil as soon as possible.

• Failure to mask the underside of the cylinder hold-down flange prior to painting the base area with orange, yellow, or green paint (to indicate the barrel type) is a major cause of inflight cylinder loss. A thin paint film under the base flange will cause torque to be lost on hold-down bolts, resulting in the studs shearing under high load. The same goes for RTV-type sealants, which should never be used under cylinder hold-down flanges.

• Pistons should not be cleaned in soap or detergent solutions. Cast aluminum is porous and will retain soap residue. Later, the soap will combine with the mineral oil in the engine to create foam, which interferes with lubrication.

• Using STP as a build-up oil can hinder break-in. STP contains a potent anti-wear agent that bonds to steel and may interfere with ring seating. Non-detergent 50- or 60-weight engine oil should be used during the final build-up.

• Chromed cylinders can be rechromed.

• Installing chromed rings (normal for a steel barrel) in chrome-plated cylinders is a mistake.

• New barrels can be put on old cylinder heads, and vice versa.

• Installing rings with the incorrect part number is a frequent error. Consult the latest manufacturer's service bulletin on ring application when choosing replacement parts.

• Beware of a failure to retorque the crankcase through studs after removal of the cylinders for top overhaul (before reinstallation). Keeping torque on these studs is necessary to prevent possible main-bearing distress.

• Connecting rods and crankshaft dynamic counterweights can be serviced during a top overhaul. If you wish to rebush rods or counterweights or replace connecting rod bolts, now is a good time to do it.

• Costly errors in craftsmanship include failure to use a fiber or wooden drift to pound piston pins out of pistons and failure to support the connecting rod properly before pounding the piston pins (allowing the crankshaft to absorb all the pounding). If the piston pins are tight, their removal can be eased by first heating the piston dome with a portable hair drier.

• Valve guides should be replaced *before* cylinder honing. Residual honing oil can cook to varnish on cylinder walls as the jug is heated in the oven in preparation for guide replacement. This varnish, in turn, will interfere with ring seating during break-in.

• It *is* often necessary to remove the entire exhaust system (and/or intake system) from an engine in order to get just one cylinder off. Your A&P isn't pulling your leg when he makes this claim.

During the buildup, care must be taken not to touch polished steel parts with bare hands which can convey corrosive salts and acids to the metal. As soon as possible, coat bare steel parts with heavyweight mineral oil.

• Cessna's labor flat-rate book recommends allowing six hours' removal/installation time for removing the first cylinder from a six-cylinder engine, then three hours more for each cylinder after that.

To Top or Not to Top: Summation

So when the possibility of a top overhaul enters the picture or when the choice appears to be between a top and a major overhaul, some basic principles should guide your thinking. First, if it's just a matter of whether even a top overhaul is necessary—

1. Do not consider a "top overhaul" unless you are personally convinced that one or more cylinders is/are mechanically or materially defective.

2. Seek advice from someone you trust (face to face), preferably someone who will not profit from a decision to go ahead with the overhaul.

3. Get a second opinion.

4. Never tear a cylinder (or engine) down on the basis of any single compression check. Employ a variety of indicators (oil consumption, spectrum analysis, compression, aircraft performance, spark plug deposits, borescope examination, etc.) as crosschecks of each other, and study the *trend,* not the individual data points.

5. Don't buy more work than you actually need. If one cylinder needs work, rework just that cylinder—not *all* the cylinders. And if the only thing a cylinder needs is new rings and a hone job, have just that work done. Don't let anyone talk you into trading your existing cylinders over overhauled/exchange units, if your present jugs are serviceable (or can be made serviceable). Likewise, if something is working okay, leave it alone; for example, don't replace the valves if they have been working all along.

6. Be sure you get what you pay for. Ask to have all replaced parts (pistons, rings, valve guides, or whatever) returned to you upon completion of the job, so you can see for yourself that your old parts really did need replacing. And inspect the *new* parts yourself, if you can, before they are installed to see that they correspond with what's shown on the final invoice.

If it develops that a thorough top overhaul (involving all cylinders) is truly in order, careful consideration should be given to performing a major, rather than a top, overhaul—particularly if the engine is more than two-thirds of the way to TBO. The reason: The difference between a thorough top and an actual major is often only $2,000 or $3,000. (The downtime difference is often negligible.) This difference is actually less than the increase in resale value of your plane that will take place after the engine is declared "zero SMOH." So it may actually pay you to do the major, rather than the top.

Another thing to consider: Most major overhauls come with a warranty. Most tops don't.

Before chroming is done, the non-chromed areas, the heads, are masked by being dipped in wax. These jugs, fresh from chroming, will be dipped in boiling water to remove the wax.

And how would you feel if—100 hours after paying $1,000 per jug for a top overhaul—your crankcase were to crack?

Remember, too, that when your engine finally does come in for its major overhaul, most of the things replaced during your top overhaul—piston rings and gaskets, for example (and maybe also exhaust valves, valve springs, etc.)—will have to be replaced again, whether they have acquired 100 hours or 1,000. (Gaskets, rings, and valve guides are mandatory-replacement items during any major overhaul.)

These are just a few of the things to consider before deciding whether to invest in a "hot section" repair to your piston engine, or go all the way with a major overhaul. The final choice is up to you.

THE POST-TOP BREAK-IN

As any accomplished burglar knows, any break-in worth doing is worth doing well.

That certainly applies to aircraft engines during the sensitive period between a top overhaul and the resumption of normal operation. Post-top break-ins are delicate matters, because various forces and factors come into play, not the least of which is that not all top overhauls are the same. The track of questions therfore begins with, Just what sort of top overhaul was performed? Which parts were affected?

Here is a representative situation and possible tacks stemming from it to ponder:

How does one "break in" an aircraft engine after, say, a ring job on two cylinders? Do you switch to mineral oil? Should you keep using ashless dispersant oil, but fly at high power settings? (How high is high? Full throttle? Top-of-the-green?) How long should it take to "seat" a new set of rings? How do you know when an engine has finally broken in?

First things first. Whenever any cylinder is reworked—for valves, guides, barrel deglazing, or whatever—the rings should be 100-percent replaced (with darn few exceptions). And whenever rings are replaced, the new ones need to be broken in. In effect, you need to break in your engine all over again—even if only one cylinder has been reworked.

What Break-in Is Meant to Do

What exactly is "break-in"? Basically, it's nothing more than the wearing away of the highest high points (microscopic ridges in the metal that look like mountains under magnification) on the surfaces of any two metal pieces that rub together. In a chrome cylinder, you're wearing cast-iron rings against a chrome-surfaced barrel; in a steel jug, you're wearing chrome-faced rings against a steel barrel.

During break-in, the very high pressure on the individual metallic ridges, as they come in contact, effectively ruptures the oil film that separates them. The resulting friction causes the highest ridges to melt and flow (or weld and unweld) in such a way as to conform to each other; the metal parts "seat" to each other. Paradoxically, an oil with anti-scuff agents (or super-high-film-strength lubricants) in it actually interferes with break-in, by preventing metal/metal contact. For this reason, it's important that molybdenum disulfide, zinc dithio-phosphate (ZPD), TCP, and other "extreme pressure" or boundary lubrication additives not be used for break-in. (Many shops unwittingly use STP, which contains ZPD, as a buildup oil to coat engine parts on assembly. This is probably a bad practice and may be why some 3 out of 10 aircraft engines fail to break in completely after overhaul.)

The oil to use for break-in is straight, unadulterated mineral oil. Texaco mineral oil is said by some mechanics to contain the fewest additives: but Aero Shell in the red can is also an industry favorite.

There are exceptions: Some engines (e.g., Lycoming O-320-H, TO-

360-C, and TIO-541 series) must start out on ashless dispersant oil, to ensure adequate lubrication of critical valve and/or turbo parts. (See Lycoming Service Bulletin No. 318, and Service Instruction 1014.)

Merely flying on mineral oil does not guarantee good break-in; high cylinder mean effective pressures are also needed to promote rupture of the ring/piston oil film. Translated, that means you have to fly at high power settings.

From the moment a fresh cylinder is put into service, the minute valleys in the surface of the metal begin to fill up with varnish (cooked oil). When the valleys overflow with varnish, the metal acquires a smooth, "glazed" surface, rendering further break-in difficult, if not impossible.

If you think about what's going on, it should be fairly evident that the process of ring seating is actually a race between the countervailing forces of ridge wear-down, on the one hand, and varnish accumulation, on the other hand. The kinetics of these two processes determine whether you end up with glazed cylinders (and 3-hrs/qt oil consumption), or good ring seating (and dry-running cylinders).

Most aircraft engines have two compression rings, an oil control ring, and (in some cases) a wiper ring below the wrist pin. Optimum oil control depends on proper break-in of all three (or four) rings. But notice what happens when you put a fresh set of rings in service: The top ring, naturally, is exposed to the greatest combustion pressure. The normal pathway for escape of the pressure is for gases to travel *behind* the rings, then down to the next land or groove; then around the inside of *that* ring, and down again. The net effect is that the number-two compression ring "feels" only about 40 percent as much pressure as the top ring; while the oil-control ring may feel only a *tenth* the pressure of the top ring. Also, there's a corresponding temperature gradient: The top ring runs hot, the second ring a little less so, and so on. What this means, of course, is that the top ring breaks in preferentially over the remaining rings in the set.

The top compression ring is going to break in no matter how you operate the engine (within reason). *But the down-stream rings may never break in, if they fail to be exposed to high pressures and temperatures.* This is why overhaulers tell plane owners not to "baby" their engines during break-in—especially low-compression types, which barely produce enough pressure below the top ring to favor good break-in even at 75 percent.

Recommended Procedures

The fact is, if you insist on performing lengthy or repeated ground runs prior to your first post-overhaul flight, you'll only hasten the formation of cylinder varnish, while creating conditions that favor the break-in of your top compression rings *to the exclusion of all other rings.* The country's largest overhaulers recommend the following procedure:

1. Pre-oil the engine before startup, in accordance with manufacturer's recommendations. (If OAT is below freezing, preheat engine and oil.)

2. Keep ground running to a minimum (5 minutes max).

3. Don't cycle the prop.

4. Take off at full power, noting rpm, oil pressure.

5. Leave the cowl flaps open. Do not reduce power to below 80 percent.

6. Climb no higher than 5,000 feet. Fly around the airport at *no less than 75-percent power* for an hour.

7. Land and check oil consumption.

How do you know when the engine has broken in? Initial ring seating should occur within the first 15 minutes to two hours. (Thereafter, cylinder head temperatures will stabilize—but remember, your factory CHT is wired to only one cylinder.) Final break-in—signified by stabilized oil consumption—should come in 50 hours.

"If oil consumption hasn't stabilized in 100 hours," says a spokesman for a respected east-coast overhaul shop, "further action — possibly deglazing of the cylinders—is called for."

Not all engines break in at the same rate (chromed jugs take a little longer than steel, for example), nor with the same degree of success. Such engines as the Lycoming O-360-A series with nitrided jugs can be counted on to break in properly, within 50 hours, in a high percentage of cases. On the other hand: "About three out of every ten O-470s we rebuild come back with break-in problems, typically high oil usage," reports one east-coast overhauler. "It has to do with ring design and operator practice, we think."

Overhaulers stress one point over and over again: Owners should not fly at reduced power during break-in. "It's the most frequent problem we have," says one A&P. "Guys are afraid to run at 26-square, or at redline. These engines are built to run wide open. But just try to convince an owner of that."

Obtaining the proper asperity during chroming is critical, for the asperities, or "channels," in the chrome surface hold the oil for cylinder-wall lubrication. As shown here, the cylinders soak in hot chromic acid at a high current for eight hours, at the end of which the current is reversed to cause the oil-holding channels to form.

Some Continental factory reps even recommend leaving the throttle firewalled on climbout, and reducing prop rpm only. (This is for low-compression, normally aspirated models.)

"Basically, you can operate your manifold pressure and rpm anywhere where there's not a red line on the gages," remarked one engine man. "Frankly, I wish more pilots would take this to heart."

Break-in After Chroming

When the engine is chromed, break-in has to be handled with special care to meet special demands. "Chrome has very poor wettability," an expert on the subject explains, "and oil control is a real problem if the asperity isn't right." (In the chroming process—which takes eight hours or more—the electric current is reversed during the last few minutes of plating. This causes tiny fissures or asperities— "channels"—to open up in the surface of the chrome.) "The degree of channeling is critical, because it's the channels that hold oil and provide proper cylinder-wall lubrication."

Break-in is often difficult in a chromed engine because the chrome *is* so hard. During break-in in a plain-steel cylinder, the rings are of harder face material than the cylinder walls, and in effect the walls seat to the rings, just as the rings seat to the cylinder. In a chromed jug, on the other hand (where soft cast-iron rings are used), the cylinder walls are extremely hard and "ungiving"; the rings seat to the walls, but not vice-versa. If the wall finish is too rough or non-uniform, the choke contour is not right, etc., the rings never stand a chance of breaking in right. "If the asperity is wrong, or the operator doesn't fly the engine hard right away, you'll get cylinder glazing before ring seating can occur," our expert affirms. "Then you're looking at pulling the jugs off, honing them, putting new rings on, and pulling your hair out. And when you're all done, you *still* might only get a quart every four hours over the life of the engine."

What's the best way to break in a freshly chromed engine? George Altgelt, one of the fathers of chrome-plating, recommends the following procedure:

1. Verify cooling baffles present and in good condition.

2. Pre-lube the engine by removing all top spark plugs (and lower plug leads) and cranking with the starter until the oil pressure gage responds. The prop will turn over very quickly because of the lack of compression with spark plugs removed.

3. In cold weather, ensure that the engine and oil are at 80° Fahrenheit before proceeding.

4. Start the engine and maintain 1,200 to 1,400 rpm for three to five minutes. Observe for leaks, unusual noises, etc.

5. Go fly. Do not cycle the propeller before takeoff, and do not accept a hold for takeoff.

6. Make a shallow climb at full power. On leveling off, fly 30 minutes at maximum cruise power.

Straight mineral oil should be used unless the engine manufacturer advises otherwise (as, for example, in the case of the Lycoming TIO-541 engine).

ECI's Jimmy Tubbs adds that he advises customers to *tow the plane to the takeoff end of the runway.* "You want to minimize unnecessary ground operation," Tubbs explains. "We literally tell people to start the engine, run it at idle for two minutes, shut down and check for leaks, then—if everything's still 'go'—tow the plane to the end of the runway, start up, and fly. Leave the prop governor alone, and if you need to check the magnetos, do it on the rollout."

Some of the drawbacks of chrome (in terms of unpredictable break-in) could no doubt be overcome if the wettability of the chrome surface could be improved. Fortunately, there may be hope. In other industries and for other applications, techniques have been perfected for suspending oil-wettable particles in the chrome plating. If applied to aircraft cylinder plating, these techniques could render old-fashioned "channel-chroming" obsolete.

Until then, chroming remains an attractive alternative to outright cylinder replacement, with special added benefits for "infrequent fliers" worried about corrosion and wear (and desert operators worried about abrasion). Just be sure your overhauler stands ready to make good on an oil-burner, in the event the break-in is poor.

It should be readily apparent by now to those newly exploring the mysteries of aircraft engines that a little savvy about the world of the cylinder can be beneficial. The more knowledge the better, especially if protective maintenance is on the agenda. Providing such information, even risking some repetition of crucial points, is the agenda of the next and following chapters.

Chapter 2

COMPRESSION, CHOKE, AND HEADS

Among the phenomena surrounding cylinder problems, real and suspected, compression anomalies, choke loss and head separation create especially troublesome headaches and confusion for concerned owners. False alarms about them occur almost as frequently as real malfunctions and are problems in themselves, for they often lead to unnecessary groundings and maintenance costs. Ignorance and sales hype tend to imbue compression evaluation and choke and head loss with a misplaced aura of mystery, which we intend here to dispel.

COMPRESSION TESTING AND EVALUATION

As was pointed out in chapter 1, compression testing can be manipulated to come up with nearly any reading desired at the time. And indeed, many mechanics handle it that way. The sharp A&P realizes (as many pilots do not) that by jogging the prop back and forth, or by squirting oil into the cylinders from a squirt-can, or by tweaking the tester's inlet pressure, or letting a cylinder cool off (or warm up) before retesting, a marginal cylinder can be made acceptable for purposes of an annual inspection—or (conversely) a 65/80 cylinder can be made the stuff of a top overhaul. Just like that. No muss, no fuss. Little wonder that compression testing is a favorite tool of the perfidious powerplant mechanic.

To be fair, by no means does misguidance come entirely from dishonesty. Mechanics do make honest mistakes, equipment does test inaccurately, and there is little or no standardized information for reference purposes to guide mechanic and owner alike.

Compression testing is a valuable preventive maintenance tool—when used knowledgeably. Unfortunately, many pilots are inexcusably naive on the subject. Many pilots believe that cylinder compression is a measure of overall engine health; that whenever a jug goes below 60/80, it must (by regulation) be removed for repair; that new cylinders, with new valves, etc., test 80/80 (or at least higher than old cylinders); that compression tends to go down over the life of an engine; and that two mechanics, testing the same engine, will usually come up with the same compression scores. All of these beliefs happen to be false.

Simple Procedure

Compression testing is a very simple procedure (any pilot can do it, with a minimum of equipment), based on some very simple principles. In a piston engine, the amount of power produced on the power stroke of each piston is proportional to the combustion pressure developed on ignition of the fuel/air charge. Combustion pressure, likewise, is a function of ring and valve sealing—the more leakage there is in these areas, the less the combustion pressure. Compression testing is merely a technique for measuring the amount of leakage in the combustion chamber.

There are two methods (and two types of apparatus) for checking

The two gages on the differential compression tester indicate input and cylinder pressures and are connected to each other in series. They are separated by a .040-inch restrictor orifice. Cylinder pressure will seem to decrease if the orifice begins to plug with dirt and/or condensation. Although the FAA does make stipulations about the configuration of the orifice, it does not require periodic calibrations of compression testers.

compression: the *direct* method and the *differential* method. A direct-type cylinder compression tester is simply a gage and a piece of tubing that connects to the cylinder. Once hooked up, the engine is turned over with the starter (or run at idle) and cylinder compression is read directly off the gage. This technique, widely practiced in automotive circles (especially with diesel engines), measures the peak pressure developed by a cold cylinder, using the engine's own intake system as the air source. It gives widely varying results, depending on engine type, compression ratio, intake system design, and, of course, the rpm developed during cranking. Thus, a compression score that might be considered "normal" for one type of engine with this prcedure might well be "abnormal" for another type of engine.

A more precise method of checking top-end tightness is afforded by the differential compression test, which is where "source" air is delivered at a precise, known pressure to the cylinder, and the amount of air *retained* in the cylinder is displayed on a second gage or dial. The difference between the source air (80 psi, usually) and the retained air (something less than 80 psi) is thus a quantitative measure of air leakage past rings and valves. If a cylinder will hold, say, 60 psi of air steadily while 80-psi input air is fed into it, the cylinder is said to have a compression score of 60/80. Since each jug is tested at the same air pressure (80 psi), all of an engine's cylinders can be checked under nearly identical conditions and meaningful comparisons are much harder to make. You can detect a bad jug by either technique. But the differential method allows finer distinctions.

The differential test apparatus is simple in design. (See *Trade-A-Plane* for names of suppliers). It consists of little more than two pressure dials connected in series, separated by a restrictor orifice, with a regulator valve upstream of both. A special air-chuck adapter that screws into 18mm spark plug bosses is included with most differential testers. To connect the tester to the cylinder, you simply remove one spark plug, insert the adapter in its place, and snap the tester onto the adapter.

A word of caution on shopping for compression testers. The FAA, in Advisory Circular 43.13-1A (p. 273), has something to say about the configuration of the restrictor orifice in the test apparatus. (The size and shape of this restrictor can have a profound effect on the results of any compression test.) For engines of less than 1,000 cubic inches' displacement, the restrictor is to have a .040-inch orifice diameter, .250-inch long, with a 60-degree approach angle. (For larger engines, the orifice should be .060-inch wide.) By all means be sure to check with the firm or persons supplying your test apparatus to be sure these specs are met.

The Procedure

The Big Two engine manufacturers and the FAA agree that compression checks should be performed with the engine hot, for optimum ring and valve sealing. (Continental Service Bulletin M73-19 states that the test should be done "as soon as possible after the engine is shut down to ensure that the piston rings, cylinder walls, and other engine parts are well lubricated.")

The test procedure is as follows:

1. After removing the most accessible spark plug (usually the top plug) from each cylinder—and after disconnecting the ignition leads from the other spark plugs, to prevent accidental firing—rotate the propeller by hand in the normal direction of rotation until the compression stroke is reached. (Put your thumb over the open spark plug hole and feel for building pressure as the piston comes up on the compression stroke.)

2. Install an adapter in the cylinder to be tested, and connect the compression tester to the adapter.

3. Checking to be sure the tester's air cutoff valve is *closed*, connect a source of clean, dry air (100-psi minimum) to the test apparatus. Tip: Be sure there's a storage tank in the system. If you try connecting directly to a compressor, the "source" air will be unsteady, and the tester's dials will quivver.

4. Locate TDC (top dead center) of the piston on the cylinder being tested. To do this, open the tester's cutoff valve until 15 to 20 psi of compressed air is being retained in

Schematic of a typical differential pressure compression tester.

the cylinder, then carefully rotate the prop in the normal direction, against the 20-psi pressure, until a "flat spot" or rapid falloff in turning resistance is encountered. Should you go beyond TDC—that is, if the prop starts to turn by itself—back up a half-revolution and try it again. You want the piston rings to be at the bottom of their lands for the test, and you want the piston itself to be at the top of its travel. If you go past top center, you'll unseat the rings. ("This is critical," Continental bulletin M73-19 reiterates, "because the slightest movement breaks the piston ring seating and allows the pressure to drop.")

5. With the prop secured (a second person should hold it steady), open the tester's air valve and adjust the unit to give an indication of 80-psi on the first gage. Use caution, since if the prop is nudged it will quickly begin turning and bang the living daylights out of whatever— or whomever—is in its way. (The reason all compression testing is done at 80 psi, incidentally, rather than a higher value—which might give more accurate results—is that 80 is as high a pressure as you can feed into the cylinder and still safely handle the prop.) Gently bump the prop back and forth a fraction of an inch if pressure indications are not steady on the second air gage. If necessary, readjust the input air to 80 psi. *Use caution at all times, making sure that nearby tools, stools, arms, legs, etc. are not in the way of the prop.*

At this point, you can take your best reading from the compression tester—and repeat the above steps for each cylinder in turn. (Be sure to make accurate notes of which compression score goes with which

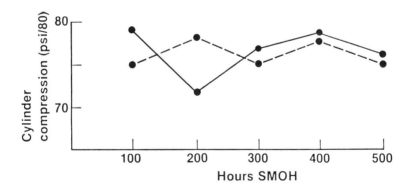

A typical compression-versus-time plot for two cylinders of a Continental IO-360-KB engine, covering 591 hours of operation. The dashed line is cylinder number 3; the solid line is cylinder number 2.

cylinder. Note that Lycoming and Continental number their cylinders differently: Lycoming starts with the crank throw closest to the prop hub, while Continental begins numbering with the cylinder closest to the copilot. One bank of jugs is odd-numbered; the other, even-numbered.)

Evaluating the Results

After doing a compression check, you'll have a string of numbers (76/80, 70/80, 72/80, etc.), all fairly close in magnitude. Or so you hope.

The question is: What constitutes a "passing score"? Some principles mentioned in chapter 1 bear repeating here. Obviously, if any cylinder has zero compression, or almost no compression (e.g., 20/80), you've got a problem. But what about borderline cases? Where do you draw the line? The FAA, as it turns out, merely states that "a loss in excess of 25 percent of the input air pressure is cause to suspect the cylinder of being defective." (See AC 43.13-1A, p. 274.) In other words, if the input air pressure is 80 psi, the minimum acceptable score is 60/80. (An exception: Tiara-series Continental engines, in which—according to TCM bulletin M76-18, Rev. 1—individual cylinder scores as low as 55/80 are considered normal.)

Mechanics and shops across the country have generally taken the above rule of thumb—which is all it is, no more—as a hard-and-fast rule requiring the removal or replacement of any cylinder showing less than 60/80. The fact of the matter, however, is that *neither the FAA nor the engine manufacturers stipulate that a cylinder below 60/80 must be removed from service.* There simply is no rule *requiring* the removal of a "low" jug.

Both Lycoming and Continental recommend against removing "low" cylinders on the basis of a single compression test. Avco Lycoming (in Service Instruction No. 1911) puts it this way: "A difference of 10 to 15 psi [between any two cylinders] indicates an investigation should be made;" however, "Unless the pressure difference exceeds 15 psi, the investigation should not necessarily mean removal of the cylinder [since] often a valve will reseat itself and result in acceptable compression during a later check, which should be made within the next ten hours of operation."

Our recommendation again—which is consistent with those of the engine manufacturers, most FAA inspectors, and many of the nation's best-known overhaulers—is to do nothing at all until a cylinder goes below 60/80; to continue to fly the engine and recheck it every 10 to 20 hours, if compression is 50/80 or above; and—in any case—to borescope cylinders before removing them. Rings rotate in their lands (alternately staggering and aligning their end gaps), and valves develop deposits that burn off and go away, etc., resulting in compression scores that wander up and down as much as 10 or 20 points in the space of 25 or 50 hours of operation. This is normal.

Actually, compression scores can wander considerably more than plus or minus 20 points; we've known jugs to go from normal (76/80) to *zero*, and back again, in the space of a few minutes. As one mechanic told us: "We saw a Bonanza one time, with a new engine, that had zero compression on one jug when it came in for a 100-hour. We ran the engine, checked it again, and it had normal compression. Ran it, checked it *again*, and it had *no* compression—which is when we knew something was definitely haywire. Well, we took the jug off and found that the exhaust valve had got to wobbling around so bad in its guide, that it only seated 'true' about every other power stroke. We replaced the valve guide, which was badly tuliped."

For a variety of reasons, the cylinder that was your highest-scoring jug at 100 hours may well be your lowest jug at 200 hours—and vice versa. Cylinder compression doesn't necessarily follow a steady pattern. (You can verify this by pulling your engine logbooks and plotting cylinder compression against time-in-service for all of your cylinders. Chances are, the final graph will look somewhat jagged.) With new engines in particular, compression scores will drift up and down as valves and rings shift and begin to seat, etc. For this reason, cylinder compression is *not* routinely checked on new engines at the factory. (Oil consumption is checked; cylinder compression is not.) In fact, you'll often find that brand-new engines have one or more jugs in the sixties or low seventies.

All of which is by way of saying that a *single* compression test doesn't necessarily mean much (just as a single oil analysis doesn't tell you much). *No* single diagnostic test should be used as the sole basis for deciding an engine's—or a cylinder's—state of health; rather, a combination of techniques should be used (over a length of time) to arrive at a final conclusion.

If your shop or mechanic doesn't agree with this, you may be able to save yourself a lot of grief—and money—by finding it out *before* your next 100-hour or annual inspection...and taking your business elsewhere.

Dealing with Low Compression

Let's say that after performing a differential compression check, you come across one jug that's in the 50s (55/80, say). What do you do?

First off, you do *not* summarily ground the airplane, unless you have other reasons for believing the cylinder in question to be defective.

The best thing to do is simply run the engine up on the ground for a few minutes (or fly around the pattern), shut her down, and recheck the cylinder. It's possible that the cylinder just wasn't hot enough the first time you checked it, or that the cylinder walls were dry—or any number of other things.

On rechecking any cylinder, it is important to listen for the sound of escaping air at the oil filler tube, the exhaust pipe, and/or the intake airbox. (Use a piece of hose, if necessary, as a stethoscope.) If you can hear air at the exhaust pipe, leakage is occurring at the exhaust valve. If you hear hissing in the induction air-scoop, leakage is occurring at the *intake* valve.

Hissing at the oil filler tube (or inside the crankcase) is indicative of ring blowby. (Hissing between cylinder cooling fins indicates real trouble: a cracked jug.) Of all these possibilities, valve leakage is most common.

Quite often, excess leakage by the piston rings can be "cured" (for purposes of the compression test) by squirting oil liberally around the piston's crown, aiming through a spark plug hole. This will help assure positive ring-to-barrel sealing. You should get a higher compression reading after applying this technique. If not, your rings may have rotated to a gaps-aligned configuration (or they may be broken); or the cylinder wall may be scored. Or your piston may be burned, or holed. A borescope examination would be the next logical step, although here again, the results are not always conclusive.

Valve leakage can sometimes be cured by staking the valve(s). To do this, first rotate the crankshaft 180 degrees, to bring the piston to bottom dead center on the power stroke. (This is a precaution designed to prevent the valves from contacting the piston during the following steps.)

Next, remove the rocker cover from the cylinder head. Then place a fiber drift on the rocker arm directly above the valve stem and deal the drift several smart blows with a 16-ounce hammer. (Repeat for the other valve.) This will dislodge any foreign matter (carbon, lead, etc.)

caught between the valve face and the valve seat.

After staking the valves, it's best to turn the engine over several times to reseat the valves before rechecking compression.

Note: If the compression scores for all of your cylinders are lower than you feel they ought to be, suspect dirt or water in the compression tester's restrictor orifice. As stated before, the size and shape of this orifice is critical. Anything that tends to make it smaller (and remember, a .040-in. hole does tend to gum up fairly easily) will make your engine's test scores low. Conversely, if you decide to clean the restrictor by reaming it out with an ice pick, you'll magically make your engine's compression go up.

Compression testing is so sensitive to equipment conditions and testing technique that it makes sense for owners who are able to do so to carry their own test equipment to a 100-hour (or annual) inspection, to make a backup check of the shop's equipment.

At the very least, any compression test that yields questionable scores should be repeated—preferably by another person, using different equipment—before jumping to conclusions. And even then, a borescope examination (if not several hours of flying) should precede cylinder removal.

Just as a score of 64/80 doesn't necessarily mean that a cylinder is mechanically defective, a *high* score—ironically—need not always mean that a cylinder is mechanically sound, either. As one Lycoming service publication points out, "Combustion chambers with five piston rings tend to seal better than three or four piston rings, with the result that the differential [compression test] does not consistently show excessive wear or breakage where five piston rings are involved."

Thus, as with oil analysis and the reading of spark plug electrodes, compression testing is most meaningful when used as an adjunct to other diagnostic techniques. Compression scores are best viewed in the presence of oil-consumption data, cockpit observations, oil analysis, and other cross-checkable inputs regarding engine health. It's the preponderance of evidence that counts (more so than the individual observations taken), not the occasional stray data point.

For all its limitations, cylinder compression testing (as described here) remains one of the best, most cost-effective preventive-maintenance procedures available to plane owners. The better you understand the technique—and its many fine points—the more money you stand to save on engine work over the long haul.

CYLINDER CHOKE

The word "choke" has an entirely different meaning in the context of aircraft engines than it does in common automotive usage. In cars, the choke is the extra carburetor butterfly that allows your engine to

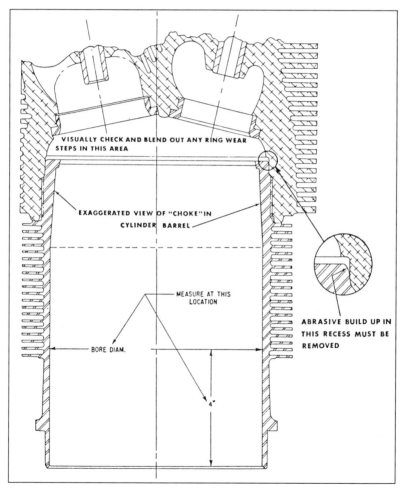

VISUALLY CHECK AND BLEND OUT ANY RING WEAR STEPS IN THIS AREA

EXAGGERATED VIEW OF "CHOKE" IN CYLINDER BARREL

MEASURE AT THIS LOCATION

BORE DIAM.

ABRASIVE BUILD UP IN THIS RECESS MUST BE REMOVED

4"

The actual choke tapering, exaggeratedly shown in this drawing, is relatively slight, but it does counter the "tulip-out" effects that could be caused by the very high temperatures that develop along the barrel during engine operation.

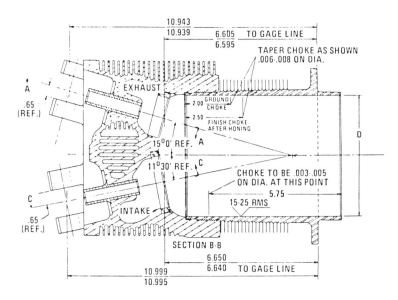

The tolerances under which cylinders operate are small and vital. The Continental TSIO-520 Overhaul Manual stipulates choke limits of .0003- to .005-inch for new jugs. [Continental diagram]

start on cold mornings. In aircraft, choke is the difference between normal TBO and a premature top overhaul.

In an aircraft-engine cylinder, when the crankcase end points up, the cylinder walls taper toward the "head" end of the barrel. This taper is the cylinder's "choke."

Why taper a barrel this way? In an air-cooled engine, a fairly extreme temperature gradient exists from the base of the cylinder to the head during normal operation. Thus, if the cylinder barrel did *not* incorporate a slight taper when cold, it would assume a negative taper or "tulip out" when hot due to thermal expansion at the combustion end). This, in turn, would lead to irregular, rapid ring wear, poor oil control, and loss of combustion efficiency. This is why new Lycoming and Continental cylinders leave the factory with as much as .010-inch taper at the head end of the barrel.

It doesn't take much choke to do the job. The Continental TSIO-520 Overhaul Manual, for example, lists acceptable choke limits of three to five thousandsths of an inch (.003- to .005-in.) for new jugs and as little as one thousandth for in-service cylinders. Lycoming's direct-drive Table of Limits doesn't contain new-limits choke specs, but *does* set a service limit of .0045-in. (four-and-a-half thou) on old barrels.

A taper of five measly thousandths of an inch on a barrel with a diameter of 5.25 inches isn't much (less than a tenth of a percent difference), but it's important for optimum ring performance. Cylinder walls that aren't parallel cause rings to wear quickly at the face, seal poorly, and flex extensively (which in turn makes for rapid land wear in the piston). Flexing, of course, is one thing brittle cast-iron rings definitely don't need.

When a cylinder comes off an engine for inspection or overhaul, a dimensional check is quickly performed. Choke is one of the essential components of this check (the others are out-of-roundness and bore); it's one of the first things the repairman looks at. It's also one of the first things that go sour when a cylinder begins to wear out. Often, a jug's bore and roundness will be well within service limits, but when the mechanic goes to check the choke—it's gone. Technically, the cylinder then becomes a reject. (It can be salvaged, of course, by reginding.) You often hear mechanics speak of engines that "won't hold the choke..." (Continental's TSIO-520s, in the steel-barreled version, are occasionally mentioned in this light, for example). This is what they're talking about.

Step Wear

Exactly how much choke a new or newly overhauled barrel should have is a favorite subject of argument among mechanics. Half the mechanics you may talk to will say that three to five thousandths (or whatever is given in the manufacturer's Table of Limits) is fine; the other half will say five thou simply is not enough. "You take a cylinder off a Pressurized Centurion engine at 700 hours," a Kansas-based overhauler once maintained, referring to the Continental TSIO-520-P used in pre-1982 P210s, "and there's *no way* you're gonna be able to legally put that jug back on without reworking it. The choke will be *gone*, man. Choke's the first thing to go on a large Continental."

Why does the choke disappear? Because the choke region is also the area of highest wear—where rings reverse travel. Lubrication is tenuous in this area because of the high wall temperatures and extreme pressure at the ring contact point. After a TBO cycle or two, it's not at all unusual to find a wear step at this cylinder depth. Not only is the choke gone—it may actually be negative. At this point, returning the proper choke contour to the cylinder may mean taking so much metal off the rest of the barrel I. D. (inside diameter) that the barrel (after grinding) may fall outside of service limits for bore. The only recourse then is to go to an oversize grind or to chrome the surface back to like-new dimensions. Both options are expensive. (Going oversize means buying a non-standard-size piston and ring set, usually costlier than normal parts. Chroming also means buying non-standard rings, in terms of metallurgy—not size.)

And guess what? Your chances of running into a choke problem (read: extra overhaul expense) are now better than ever, thanks to recent changes in the way Lycoming and Continental make cylinders.

Nitriding

In an attempt to retard cylinder wear, lengthen TBOs, and reduce warranty complaints, both Big Two engine makers have in recent years gone to nitriding cylinder barrels. Nitriding is a special surface-hardening treatment (one that can be used on most steels but works especially well with certain steel alloys containing aluminum—i.e., nitralloys) wherein steel parts are exposed to ammonia gas at high temperature, generally near 1,000° Fahrenheit. (Because the high temperatures are damaging to aluminum, nitriding is done early in manufacture, before the barrel is attached to the cylinder head.) The ammonia undergoes thermal cracking to form nitrogen and hydrogen which (in turn) impregnate the surface of the metal and harden it—but only to a depth of ten thousandths or so. (The exact depth depends on the cook time.) The advantage of nitriding from the manufacturer's standpoint is that it's cheap and easy and involves no exotic production facilities outside of a large oven. Compared to the alternatives—chrome plating, or the use of more expensive barrel alloys—nitriding is certainly the most cost-effective way to achieve a hard wear surface.

The down side is seen at overhaul time. Although nitrided steel wears slowly, it does wear down, and it definitely can rust. (Some experts contend that nitrided jugs actually rust and pit *faster* than plain steel jugs.) Eventually, a nitrided cylinder will need light grinding to restore roundness (barrels wear oval in service), remove wear steps, restore choke, etc. Unfortunately, this is where trouble begins. Nitriding produces a hardened surface layer of *uneven* thickness, perhaps no more than a few thousandths' thickness in the thinnest spots (while maybe .015-inch deep in the thickest spots). Even in areas that extend to .010 or .015-inch below the surface, the hardness of the steel decreases quite rapidly beyond .005-inch from the surface. Anything

Steel-belted pistons and reduced-choke cylinders were first introduced as a product improvement for the Cessna 421C, circa 1981.

(such as grinding) that causes the nitride layer to be breached will open up soft spots in the metal, and irregular wear will then occur.

For maintenance purposes, this means that nitrided jugs can't be ground oversize. Lycoming forbids the practice, in fact, except for low-compression O-360-B and -D and O-540-B engines (see Service Instruction No. 1047B), which may be ground to .010-over *only*. (Normally, Lycoming permits a choice of .010-over or .020-over regrinding of cylinders.) As an alternative to regrinding, Lycoming permits nitrided jugs to be chrome-plated, or rebarreled.

It also means that wear steps greater than .0025-inch (two and a half thousandths) cannot be removed from nitrided jugs by grinding. (Again, see Lycoming S. I. 1047B.) a corollary of this is that *choke* often can't be restored to a nitrided jug by regrinding.

These considerations are starting to affect many owners. All current-production Lycoming engines except O-235-C, O-320-A/C/E, and IO-320-A and -C come with nitrided cylinders (and have, for many years). If you're not sure whether your Lycoming has nitrided jugs, look at the base of the cylinder. Blue paint on the hold-down flange means the jug in question is nitrided.

Continental only recently switched from plain steel to nitrided-steel engines: TSIO-360-LB/MB, O-470-U (with 2,000-hr TBO), high-TBO (1,600-hour) TSIO520 models, and the Malibu and Crusader engines. Since Continental doesn't use blue paint to color-code its nitrided cylinders, a call to the factory may be the only way to pin down the status of some engines.

But that's not all you should know. For Continental owners, the plot thickens even further.

Steel-Insert Pistons

In recent years, a complaint heard over and over again among engine rebuilders is that the Continental factory is putting too little choke in its 470- and 520-series cylinders. "They keep putting less choke in 'em each year,' one Texas-based cylinder repair professional laments. "Now we're seeing new jugs that have no choke in 'em at all."

As the choke has disappeared, Continental has (perhaps coincidentally; perhaps not) begun phasing in a new series of piston with a cast-iron insert to hold the top compression ring. According to Continental Custom Information Bulletin CIB 85-5, the purpose of the steel insert is "to reduce ring flutter." But at least one repair shop dismisses the "ring flutter" argument as nonsense.

"With the proper choke engineered into a cylinder," says an August 1985 Customer Information Bulletin from Engine Components Inc., "so-called 'ring flutter' will not occur." What's more, "Since the correct choke/-piston/ring combination eliminates the 'ring flutter' hazard, there is no necessity for using a reinforced piston." ECI maintains that, to the extent that Continental has had some unexplained ring failures in its engines, the breakages are choke-related—that is, related to *lack* of choke. Reinforcing the piston is a Band-Aid fix, to ECI's way of thinking. Band-Aid or no Band-Aid, steel-belted pistons are not without disadvantages. For one thing, they're quite a bit heavier than standard aluminum pistons (thus increasing the engine's reciprocating mass and internal friction losses). They're also costlier than cast-aluminum pistons. (List price on Continental's steel-belted pistons comes to about $150 each—vs. $50 or so for one-piece pistons.)

More important, the latest-style steel-insert pistons *will not fit most older cylinders*. There is an interference problem between the piston crown and cylinder head. Old-style (all-aluminum) pistons for 470- and 520-series Continentals are beveled around the top of the crown; whereas for reasons unknown, Continental's new hybrid construction pistons are perfectly flat on top—not beveled. As a result, the new pistons can, at top dead center, contact the lip or head-joint overhang where the barrel meets the cylinder head—an extremely unsatisfactory situation.

Continental is aware of the interference problem. Their answer to it is to require remachining of cylinder heads (from the inside) to remove metal at the head/barrel joint prior to putting new-style pistons in service. The machining operation is spelled out in Continental Service Bulletin M85-9 (Revision1).

To say that not everyone is happy with S.B. M85-9 would be an understatement. In the first place, the bulletin makes no mention of new versus old-style pistons. In fact, no part numbers or serial numbers of any kind are mentioned. The bulletin merely requires an inspection of piston dome clearance at top or major overhaul time, to ensure an unobstructed head clearance of 0.120-inch (plus .020, minus zero) with the piston at top dead center. For effectivity, the bulletin merely lists "470, 520, and 550 series engines." In foreign countries such as Canada, where service bulletin compliance is mandated by law, operators are understandably confused. The language of M85-9 doesn't make clear the fact that *not* all 470, 520, and 550 Continentals are affected—only those that are being converted from beveled to non-beveled (latest-style) pistons. Naturally, operators of newer airplanes (1985 P210s and Malibus, for instance) are exempt since they are already using flat-topped pistons without ill effect.

Confusing matters still further is the fact that Continental's steel-insert pistons have, in some cases, already undergone P/N revisions reflecting dimensional changes. The head-clearance problem may not exist with some early-configuration hybrid pistons but only comes up when switching from early hybrid (superseded-P/N) to late hybrid (current P/N, flat-top) pistons. This is not spelled out in the bulletin.

Other Ambiguities

There are other ambiguities in the bulletin. Continental's M85-9 does not specify the tools to be used in removing cylinder-head metal, or precautions to be taken to ensure that the head-to-barrel joint tension is not accidentally disrupted in the machining process. Also, the blend radius of 0.62 of an inch given in the bulletin has no plus-or-minus tolerance. Even more important, the bulletin does not mention any method of marking or identifying the cylinder to indicate that S. B. M85-9 has been complied with.

Of course, while the bulletin doesn't say so, all of this is of academic interest only, if an operator decides to stay with old-fashioned, all-aluminum, bevel-topped pistons. Unfortunately, Continental is phasing out such pistons, and the owner who insists (at overhaul time) on using "genuine factory parts" will find it necessary to spend as much as $250 per cylinder ($150 for parts, $100 for machine work) just to replace an engine's pistons—never mind rings, valves, or guides, plus chrome-plating and/or regrinding to restore choke.

Our opinion? Stay with old-style pistons if you own a big Continental, and insist on a *minimum* of .005-inch choke in the barrel. If you can't get old-P/N pistons from Continental (and you probably won't be able to), fine. Order aftermarket pistons from ECI, Precision, Superior, or whoever makes the P/N piston your engine uses. For example, one-piece aluminum pistons for IO-520 engines can be bought, new, from ECI under P/N AEC-631475. Pistons for other engine models are available, too. (ECI, 9503 Middlex, San Antonio, TX 78286). We'd avoid using steel-insert pistons except where ring breakage and/or piston ring land wear has been a problem.

How Much Choke?

The question of exactly how much choke should be ground into your cylinders at overhaul is something you'll want to discuss with your overhaul agency. (Any agency that recommends no choke at all on a large engine should be avoided.) As stated above, five thousandths of an inch is generally a good minimum figure to shoot for, although in cases of severe wear at the top of the barrel, achieving a choke more than this may be impossible without going oversize on the main bore.

To some degree, the amount of choke you should have is dependent on the type of flying you do and the cooling ability of the engine. If you have an engine that has persistently high cylinder head temperatures in flight (perhaps you fly at 20,000 feet a good deal of the time), you'll benefit from having more choke ground into the cylinders. On the other hand, if most of your flying is done above the Arctic Circle, at low power settings, and you rarely see CHTs above the low green, you don't need much choke. Some shops recognize this and will custom-grind a customer's cylinders accordingly.

There is, of course, a practical upper limit on how much choke can be put into a cylinder. The limit is set by ring gap closure. During buildup of an engine, ring gap is usually measured by inserting the piston ring(s) a short way into the open end of the cylinder barrel and checking the distance between ends of the ring with a feeler. Typical go/no-go limits for ring gap, checked in this manner, might be .038- to .054-inch. (These numbers are in fact from the Continental O-470 Overhaul Manual.) But that's with the ring at the largest diameter point in the barrel. Scoot the same ring up into the barrel about five inches, where choke is maximal, and the gap may shrink to .010-inch or less, depending on the exact amount of choke. In some cases, the gap will close altogether. Put the ring in service, and it will break, causing extensive damage. (Ring gap is also affected by ambient temperature;

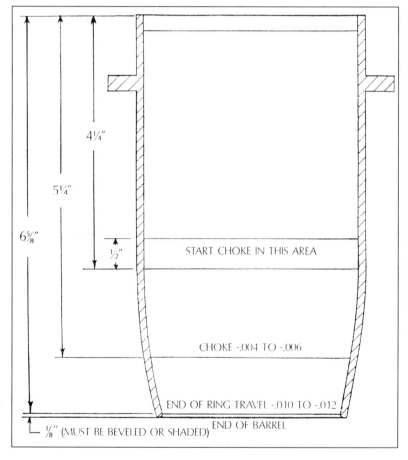

4¼"

5¾"

6⅝"

½"   START CHOKE IN THIS AREA

CHOKE -.004 TO -.006

END OF RING TRAVEL -.010 TO -.012

⅛" (MUST BE BEVELED OR SHADED)   END OF BARREL

The ring gap closure establishes the limit of the choke in a cylinder. Over the range of the tapering area, the limits can narrow considerably.

on a cold-start without preheat, what may have been a normal ring gap for a standard day could mean ring binding at five below.) This effectively puts an upper limit of about .010-inch on the choke—unless you want to cheat by filing the ends off your rings. (Use a fine file and finish by polishing the ends with an Arkansas stone.)

A difference in diameter (choke) of .010-inch converts to a .0314-inch difference in ring gap, which is a sizable variance. With engines having chokes of .001-inch to .010-inch, one might well question why the manufacturers don't require mechanics to measure ring gaps at the tightest point in the barrel (the point of greatest choke). The answer is that Continental now does require this. As of October 1, 1985, Teledyne Continental revised its ring-gap go/no-go limits (for *all* TCM engine models) to reflect the "deep throat" method of gap measurement. Under Service Bulletin M85-17, shops *must* now measure ring gaps by inserting rings to a depth of 5.75 inches in the barrel first, before reaching in with a feeler. At this depth, the go/no-go limits are .010 to .030-inch. If a ring has a gap of less than .010-inch, Continental allows filing the ends of the ring(s); if more than .030-inch, it is permissible to select from .005-oversize rings as necessary.

While the bulletin doesn't specifically say so, M85-17 appears to be a response to the chaotic situation that has developed with regard to cylinder choke. What both manufacturers (Lycoming and Continental) *should* do, we feel, is issue customer information bulletins stating in explicit terms exactly what the factory's present production tolerances are for choke (for all the various engine models), and what the new and service limits are for choke, step-wear, and reground bore on nitrided barrels. Neither Lycoming nor Continental currently publishes "new choke limits" for all engine models. And Continental has yet to make any recommendations on grinding or polishing of nitrided barrels.

Perhaps a procedure ought to be established, also, whereby shops stamp or etch the barrel choke (.005, .007, or whatever) on the outside of the cylinder somewhere, much as color-coding (and impression-stamping, in some cases) is now used to indicate the presence of oversize components. At the very least, this information ought to be recorded in the airplane's maintenance records.

In the meantime, do yourself a favor and pay attention to choke when your cylinders are off. A little knowledge of choke not only separates knowlegeable pilots (and mechanics) from the unknowledgeable, but weeds the squawk-free engines from the "problem babies." It's a fine point of engine repair that more pilots should bring under their control.

Helpful Operational Practices

There are things you can do from the operational and maintenance standpoints to help keep the choke in your barrels:

1. Don't gun the engine on startup. Keep idle speeds low until the cylinders have had a chance to warm up. Steel cylinders do not expand as much or as fast as aluminum pistons. Until those barrels warm up, your pistons will be ramming their compression rings in and out of a tapered tube; the result (if you're not careful) is apt to be a pronounced wear step where the rings reverse travel at the top of the stroke. There is no faster way to destroy choke.

2. Preheat not only your oil but your cylinders as well prior to starting your engine below 25°F. The warm-up/wear-step problem is greatly aggravated by low temperatures at startup. Not only are cylinder dimensions smaller (due to thermal contraction) but oil flows less easily, creating definite lubrication problems with the piston rings. The latter problem can be circumvented by switching to multigrade oil. But even if you're using multigrade oil, you should invest in a thorough engine preheat prior to every cold-weather start cycle, to minimize wear-step formation.

3. Use the proper grade of oil for existing ambient temperatures and change oil often. Proper attention to oil and filter maintenance is absolutely essential to the prevention of "choke loss."

CYLINDER HEAD SEPARATION

Losing your head in flight is never a good idea, but losing a *cylinder head* 10,000 feet over Kansas is bad P.R. indeed. Yet, statistics suggest that head-loss is not an unheard of problem in general aviation. In a recent five-year span, for example, over 150 Service Difficulty Reports were filed with the FAA regarding cylinder head separation in 520-series Continental engines. On average, that's a failure rate of one cylinder every 12 days—just for 520-series Continental owners alone. (Other engine types also shed heads: O-200, TSIO-360, and IO-470 owners have all been hit with head-fracture Airworthiness Directives over the years. We mention the 520 series for purposes of illustration only.)

Head loss does not always occur in mid-air, of course. "On annual inspection, found one cylinder with no compression," reads one report on an S35 Bonanza's IO-520-B. "Low compression due to No. 2 cylinder separating at head-to-barrel connection," states a report on a Baron 58. "Tapping noise in engine traced to head-to-barrel torque loose," says a report on a Cessna 185.

Nevertheless, in a sizable number of cases (around 40 percent of the total), separation occurs in fairly dramatic fashion, with little or no warning. "No. 5 cylinder on left engine came loose, blew open cowling, and knocked a hole in the left side of fuselage," observes a report on a Cessna 310R (327 hours TT). "Cylinder head separated from barrel on takeoff" on a Cessna TU206. "While in flight a large bang was heard and engine began to run rough," according to a report on a P206A, which concluded: "No. 4 cylinder head had separated from barrel." And in a U206 (IO-520-F engine): "Power loss and fire disclosed No. 5 cylinder head separated from the barrel.

Ground for the Divorce

What causes heads to detach from cylinder barrels? Are the above incidents—and hundreds of others like them—mere freak occurrences? Or are certain identifiable risk factors involved?

One possible clue to the nature of the problem is evident from cylinder anatomy. Air-cooled aircraft cylinder assemblies consist of a tubelike steel barrel (which may be chromed or nitrided, or oxide-coated, or plain on the inside diameter) joined to an aluminum-alloy *head* with large cooling fins. The alloy head (typically cast AMS 4225 aluminum, in some cases made via hot isostatic pressing, or "HIPing") screws onto the steel barrel and is locked in place by interference fit; the heated head is "shrunk" onto the refrigerated barrel, and when everything cools down, the valveless cylinder assembly—also known in the trade as a stud—can be considered to be structurally of one piece. In theory.

In reality, aluminum expands approximately twice as much as steel with exposure to heat, and the head end of the cylinder is where all the calories are. So what starts out as a sound interference fit at room temperature can become a somewhat relaxed fit at normal cylinder operating temperatures, particularly if something has been done to the cylinder assembly to diminish the head/barrel preload.

What could possibly affect the head junction preload of a cylinder in service? Not much, if the cylinder is less than one TBO run old and has never come off for maintenance. Most aircraft cylinders, however,

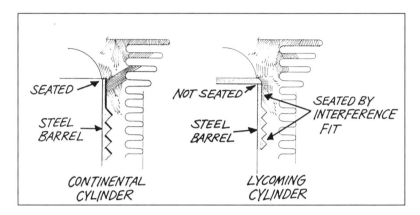

Lycoming and Continental use slightly different head retention schemes (note the slight gap formed at the barrel junction in the Lycoming jug). A process pioneered by ECI of San Antonio takes the best features of both seating methods and adds a proprietary sealant to "bond" the barrel and head together.

remain in service for several TBO runs (several thousand hours), but to make it through the third and fourth overhauls, many have to be ground oversize and chromed. Many more have to be welded to repair cracks in the head area. During these and other remanufacturing operations, cylinders are often oven-heated to temperatures over 600° Fahrenheit to relieve stresses introduced in repair operations. After repeated oven heatings, head/barrel joints can relax. But unless the head is unscrewed from the barrel, and thread dimensions are inspected (and restored as needed) before reassembly, there is no way to check the soundness of the head-barrel junction. The cylinder is simply put back in service.

And it may do just fine. By far the majority of remanufactured cylinders returned to service give satisfactory performance, with no tendency toward spontaneous disassembly in mid-air. But throw in an overboost here, a backfire there, perhaps a flooded (hydrostatic-lock) start now and again, advanced timing, a dose of bad gasoline, etc., and you begin to see where "weak" jugs get their opportunity, eventually, to pop.

Assembly and Aging

"Partly it's an age thing," one engine man (experienced in the original manufacture of cylinders) has said, referring to cylinders that blow their tops. "That junction does lose some of its original integrity with repeated thermal cycles, over the course of a couple of TBOs. There's no getting around it. A 'young' jug is going to be tighter—although you have to be sure to assemble it right to begin with. Continental had a problem some years ago with heads coming off their Skymaster engines, the IO-360s. There was a problem in assembly. You see, it was part of the required assembly procedure to butt the barrel up square against the head during the torquing—you actually would smack the barrel hard to seat it. They weren't smacking 'em, though, and after a while a whole batch of those jugs failed in service. That was the subject of an AD."

Not every Service Difficulty Report in our files gives complete information on time since overhaul, chrome versus steel, and so on, for every failed cylinder, but it is clear from a quick reading of the printouts that, first, many (if not most) of the head separations involved cylinders on second or third TBO runs—maybe fourth or fifth "top overhauls," if you consider that the typical 520 Continental jug probbly sees one removal every 800 to 1,000 hours.

It's also clear, from a quick read-through of the SDR file, that a fair number of broken cylinders failed shortly after chroming.

One way to get a handle on head junction integrity is to periodically rebarrel the cylinder—literally take it apart and inspect it. In the rebarreling process, the cylinder head and all parts of the barrel joint area are thoroughly checked *inside and out* before repair and/or reassembly. Among other things, this means that the barrel threads (which screw into the head) are checked for condition and dimensions, to ensure a positive "like new" interference fit on final reassembly. If the threaded portion will not "clean up" within appropriate limits, the barrel is rejected, or its threads ground .010 or .020-inch oversize and used with oversize heads. Lycoming rebarrels cylinders routinely at the factory (during engine remanufacture). In the field-overhaul market, Engine Components Incorporated of San Antonio is the largest rebarreler of aircraft cylinders.

What can pilots do to prevent head separation? Besides not over-boosting and avoiding hydrostatic lock, operators can grind oversize during overhaul rather than chrome-plate; and if cylinders are of questionable integrity (from sheer age, overheating, possible detonation or dubious field repairs), they should be sent out for full "demate" (rebarreling inspection) at overhaul.

When demate/remate is done, a tighter-than-new head joint can be achieved by use of an appropriate sealant in the thread area. ECI of San Antonio has developed a proprietary, FAA-approved sealant process for this purpose and claims to have achieved good success with it.

Can head separation be detected by the pilot before it progresses to an inflight failure? The FAA seems to think so. In AD 72-20-02 (on head separation in IO-470 Continentals), the FAA recommends a visual inspection of the head junction area for oil wetness. A pre-wash is advisable to remove old oil buildups; then you can run the engine up to normal operating temperatures, shut down, and observe for leakage. "During the inspection," the FAA notes, "it may also be helpful to rotate the propeller to detect *significant differences in compression* between cylinders, or audible compression leakage through a crack in the cylinder barrel." (Caution: Treat the prop as if it were hot.)

Nothing quite matches actually looking at the area for evidence of a separation drama about to unfold—or at any jug part that may become delinquent. For information about taking your cylinders in hand, please read further.

Chapter 3

CYLINDER REMOVAL AND PROBLEM DIAGNOSIS

Intrepid and experienced practitioners of light plane manintenance may or may not balk at the idea of pulling a suspect cylinder for diagnostic purposes, but many average owners no doubt will. Yet if cost savings are part of his or her agenda, a stranger to such work may want to consider it further. As one *LPM* editor discovered in the days of ascendant inflation, removing and inspecting a jug can pay dividends. The costs quoted in his account are as of December 1980, but the lessons they embody remain in force and could be even timelier tomorrow, if prices significantly inflate again.

STEP-BY-STEP REMOVAL

The handwriting had begun to appear on the wall about a year before, when the owner noticed what appeared to be a slight increase in his Continental's rate of oil consumption. Instead of getting four hours to a quart, he was suddenly getting only three. Oil analysis showed nothing unusual, so he kept flying the plane (a 1968 Cessna 182). But before long, the oil burn rate was up to a quart every two hours. Then a quart every hour and a half. Next thing he knew, his cruise airspeed was off a couple miles per hour. Spark plugs began to foul out. Something was definitely amiss.

When the top-hole plugs were removed in preparation for the differential compression check, he couldn't help noticing that several of his plugs had oily firing ends. Thus, it came as no surprise when three jugs turned up "soft" on the compression test. Cylinders two, three, and five were all below 60/80. What's more, as air was applied to each of the cylinders in turn, hissing could be heard at the oil filler cap—an indication of excessive blowby due to stuck rings and/or worn cylinder walls.

Based on any single factor alone, he probably would not have made a decision to remove the cylinders. High oil consumption (as any owner of a pre-1973 Skylane will tell you) is a natural trait of the Continental O-470-R engine. Likewise, low compression—by itself— does not justify cylinder removal (unless, of course, the compression is near zero), because low compression is often a *transient* phenomenon. Valves acquire carbon and then burn clean again, rings rotate in their grooves, etc., causing cylinder compression to fluctuate noticeably over the life of an engine.

What made him finally decide to ground the airplane—and remove the "soft" cylinders—was the *clear pattern* that was emerging, the *corroborative* nature of the data. The high oil consumption, the wet spark plugs, the reduction in cruise performance, the low compression coupled with audible hissing at the oil filler cap—all pointed in one direction. He became convinced, based on what he knew about his engine (and about Continental O-470-R's in general), that he had ring problems in three cylinders—stuck rings, more than likely—and that he'd best take the jugs off and have a look. Under the supervision of an A&P mechanic, that's exactly what he did.

"Prepping" the Engine

He had two reasons for wanting to remove (and later reinstall) the cylinders himself. One was strictly financial. The mechanic estimated the labor requirement (if he were being paid to do the job) at six hours—for cylinder *removal* only. By removing the cylinders himself, the owner stood to save at least $150 [1980 dollars—*Ed.*] on the total job—perhaps twice that if he also reinstalled the jugs.

The second reason for going the "do-it-yourself" route was educational. He had never taken the cylinders off an aircraft engine before, and he wanted to see if a totally unprepared amateur could do the job. He was to learn that the average amateur can safely handle the job, given appropriate supervision. No part of the cylinder removal process involves superhuman ability, despite what you may have heard.

In an overall sense, the cylinder removal procedure is quite straightforward. With a little common sense, you can figure it out for yourself—which is indeed fortunate, since the Continental O-470-R/IO-470-R shop manual tells absolutely nothing about how to remove cylinders from an engine that's installed in an airplane. (Don't look for this information in a Cessna manual either. It's not written down anywhere.)

Obviously, before you can actually begin removing jugs, you have to spend some time "prepping" the engine (i.e., removing cooling baffles, exhaust components, and anything else that might be in your way when it comes time to pull jugs). In this case, it meant—initially, at least—disconnecting the ducting from the heater shroud, removing the shroud itself, disconnecting ignition leads, disassembling the between-cylinders baffle plates, and loosening the intake-riser connections. Ultimately, he ended up having to remove the complete exhaust and induction manifolds. Even though he was only interested in gaining access to (and removing) cylinders two, three, and five, the construction of the intake and exhaust systems (and their mutual interference) is such that complete removal is a must. If you study your particular installation, you'll see what we mean. The exhaust riser assembly for cylinders two and six comes in one piece; you have to remove the whole thing, even if you don't care about working on cylinder number six. Ditto for the exhaust risers to jugs one and five. (Cylinders three and four have short, independent risers that attach via clamp connections to the rest of the system.)

Fortunately, the Skylane's exhaust and intake manifolds come loose quite readily if you have the proper tools. For the exhaust system, your most important tools will be [1] a spray can of WD40, Liquid Wrench, or some similar product for loosening rusty nuts, [2] A 7/16-inch flex socket on a 4-inch or longer extension. Poor access to manifold nuts (four per flange) makes the latter tool an absolute necessity. You won't be able to see what you're doing, so you might want to bring a flashlight.

Be sure to spray rusted exhaust nuts with WD40 penetrant a full minute before you begin working on them; this gives the oil time to soak in and do its job. But be ready, in any case, for unexpected problems. Don't be shocked if a stud backs out (several will). Also, don't panic if a stud breaks off. (It's not good news, but don't panic.) It can be taken care of after the cylinder is in the overhaul shop.

On some Cessnas, the entire exhaust system can be removed from the engine intact. On this one, it was necessary to uncouple one side of the muffler and remove the system in two pieces or assemblies. Seven exhaust studs backed out of their holes, but fortunately, no studs broke off. (One clamp bolt snapped in half, but it was a standard AN3 bolt, which was simple to replace.)

An O-470 cylinder with the rocker cover removed. The intake valve is on the right. To get at the pushrods, you will have to clip the safety wire on the rocker shaft retainer bolts, remove the bolts, tap the shafts sideways and lift out the rocker arms. The pushrods, which are not visible here, can then be plucked from their housings, which can be seen at the bottom of the photograph.

If you've ever studied a Continental intake manifold, you know that (unlike Lycoming intake risers, which arise independently of one another from somewhere deep in the oil sump) the components of the Continental system join together by means of rubber hoses and clamps. Between every pair of jugs is a hose and two clamps joining successive pieces of intake manifold. The clamps are easy to remove, but the hoses—which tend to harden and shrink with time—can be a pain to free up and slide back and forth. It's amazing how deteriorated these connectors can become in a few hundred hours. The owner decided to replace all the intake riser hoses. Have you looked at yours lately? You might want to do the same thing.

Pushrods, Housings

One of the final preliminaries to cylinder removal is removal of the pushrods and pushrod housings for each cylinder. This can be accomplished in about ten minutes, if you know how—and every plane owner should know how.

You start, naturally, by removing the rocker box cover from the end of the cylinder; for this, you need just a large screwdriver. (Put the fillister-head cap-screws in a small box or cup as you remove them, so they won't get lost. Note that some of the screws are longer than others.) Be ready for some oil to dribble out as you remove the valve cover.

The next thing to do is "unload" the pushrods (close both valves) by hand-turning the propeller until the compression stroke for that cylinder is reached.

Now you can—one at a time—loosen the bolt that secures each rocker shaft to its boss, tap the free rocker shaft sideways (not all the way out of its boss, but enough to liberate the rocker itself), and remove each rocker. There will be a washer on each side of each rocker; don't lose these.

With the rockers removed, you can reach your fingers into the pushrod housings and withdraw the loose rods. (The rods should be the same length, since the 470-series engines use hydraulic valve lifters. If you are working on an engine with solid tappet bodies, or for some reason your pushrods are *not* the same length, do not under any circumstances get the two rods mixed up. It's best to identify them in some way.)

To remove each pushrod housing, push the exposed end (with a blunt tool of some sort) toward the crankcase, against its spring, until the outer end (the end you're pushing on) is clear of the hole, then drop the housing out and catch the spring. Note: There will be two steel washers and a red or white Silastic seal at each end of each pushrod housing. Keep the washers and order new seals.

Now replace the rockers, rocker shafts, and hold-down bolts on the cylinder head before they all get lost.

Pulling Jugs

Once the foregoing preparatory work is out of the way, actual cylinder removal is easy. But again, you have to have the right tools— and for cylinder removal, that means cylinder base-nut wrenches of the appropriate sizes (5/8-inch and 7/16-inch, for the Continental O-470-R). Poor access may prevent you from reaching certain cylinder hold-down nuts with standard tools.

There is one possible contingency for which you definitely should come prepared any time you are removing cylinders from an engine. Some cylinder hold-down studs on some engines (the large stud at the eight o'clock position on the base flange of number four cylinder on this engine, for instance) are actually through-studs that go all the way through the crankcase. It is possible—in fact, the chances are 50-50— that when you go to remove a nut on one of these studs, the *stud will turn with the nut.*

Getting the nut off, in this case, can be difficult and may in fact pose a serious threat to your sanity. (You cannot simply choose to remove the whole stud, nut and all, due to the fact that a rubber O-ring is used at each end of the stud. If you pull the stud out, you'll drag its threaded ends across the O-rings, damaging them and creating an oil leak that— quite possibly—won't get cured until the next major overhaul.)

So here's what you do: If you suspect that a through-stud is going to turn on you, immediately drop what you're doing and figure out a way to *double-nut the opposite end of the stud.* (Cylinder-fin clearance problems may make this easier said than done, but you have no choice. Do what you have to do to get two nuts on that stud.) Only if you torque two nuts down on the opposite end of the stud can you get it to stay until you liberate the nut from the cylinder base flange you're working on. Mechanics are aware of this problem (and this solution). Call on a mechanic for help, if need be—don't be bashful.

Of course, this entire problem could have been eliminated back at the drawing board at Continental (you'd think Continental's engineers could have designed a keyed or splined crankcase through-stud, etc.)—but that's another story.

After alternately loosening—then removing—the cylinder holddown nuts for each cylinder you're working on, all you have to do is walk up to a cylinder, put your arms around it and pull. The jug will come right off in your arms. Also, the piston and connecting rod will crash right down onto the crankcase, if you let them (which you definitely should not!)—so be ready to prop the connecting rod up with a well-placed rag or two at the moment of cylinder removal. (Tip: Get someone to help you.)

After setting the cylinder in a safe place, go back and remove the piston from the rod. Tap the piston pin out with a mallet and wooden stake while a second person holds the connecting rod stationary (so that your hammering isn't "felt" by the crankshaft). When the piston pin slides out, remove the piston, put the pin back in the piston, and put both next to the corresponding cylinder.

Before you do anything else, go back to the engine and secure the loose connecting rod properly. (An improperly stowed rod can easily be nicked on the edge of the crankcase, setting up the kind of localized stress concentration that could later result in failure of the part.) The standard procedure here is to place rubber bands around the rod and cylinder hold-down studs in such a way that the rod cannot contact any sharp surfaces.

If you want to keep dirt out of your engine, you might go a step further: Obtain a large (8-inch square) piece of corrugated cardboard, cut a big "X" in the center, and make smaller X's around the periphery (one per stud); then press the whole thing over the connecting rod and all eight cylinder studs to create an effective dust shield for the big, gaping hole in the side of your engine.

PARTS CHECKS AND JUG REPLACEMENT

A completed removal places before you both an opportunity to see where the problems lie and the freedom to make some intelligent and prudent choices about solving them. This owner had a relatively simple condition to deal with, but the same advantages accrue for more complex and demanding difficulties.

Cylinder Rework

You may never know until you look inside a cylinder exactly what you're going to find. In this case, the situation became clear with an examination of the pistons and rings. As had been suspected all along, the engine had stuck rings. What's more, the rings had rotated (before sticking) to a position that allowed their end gaps to more-or-less line up, creating tremendous possibilities for blowby. Except for that, though, all components looked okay. No evidence of piston scuffing or burning was present; no rings were broken or missing; no cylinder scoring had taken place. Two barrels showed visible wear steps at the upper limit of ring travel. (This is to be expected —particularly if you have been operating with stuck rings.)

Rather than send the cylinders out to a repair facility for overhaul (which, in his opinion, they didn't need), he decided to take them to an experienced mechanic and AI whose judgment and workmanship he knew from previous experience to be unimpeachable. He had this man clean and inspect the pistons, clean and check the cylinder barrels, and check the valve guides for excessive wear. The cylinders (and pistons) proved to be serviceable, so the barrels were honed, and new rings were fitted to the pistons. The total labor tab for this came

You can facilitate reassembling the cylinders to the engine by first inserting the pistons (and the upper rings) in the jugs to the level of the piston pin with the aid of the ring compressor. You can then bring the partially assembled piston and cylinder to the engine as a unit and secure the connecting rod to the piston while the latter is in place in the cylinder barrel. The ring compressor must then be used again to fit the bottom "scraper" ring on the piston.

to 2.5 hours at $25/hour, or $62.50, much less than the $35 to $70 *per cylinder* one could have been expected to pay to have a cylinder-overhaul facility "clean up" the jugs.

The total parts cost at this point came to $239.07—including new rings, gasket sets, exhaust studs, pushrod seals, intake hoses, and miscellaneous hardware. (Impatience to get the plane flying again led to payment of full list price for all parts; had he shopped around, he no doubt could have saved another 20 percent.)

It is possible to buy a ring job for a high-performance aircraft engine for a total parts-and-labor cost of *under $110 per cylinder*, if you are willing to supply some of the labor yourself, and if you insist on repairing or replacing *only* those parts that need to be repaired.

Exactly how many $300 ring jobs get passed off on unsuspecting plane-owners as $2,000 top overhauls requiring cylinder replacement, one never knows.

Replacement Tips

Hanging new (or refurbished) jugs back on an engine is, if anything, simpler than taking them off. Basically, all you do is go through the disassembly steps in reverse order, with the following exceptions:

1. One tool you'll absolutely have to have that you didn't use before is a *ring compressor*, which you *must* use to get the pistons back in their jugs. Have a mechanic show you how to use one of these simple devices, if you've never worked with one before.

2. Getting cylinders off is—possibly—a one-man task, but putting them back on again definitely requires four hands. Don't try to do everything yourself. It won't work.

3. Did you remove all the old gaskets from your cylinder intake and exhaust port? It's easier to do this while the cylinders are removed from the engine than after hanging them back on. Intake-port gaskets, in particular, give trouble (i.e., they stick like glue). Be prepared to do some heavy-duty scraping to remove dried-out, mashed-down, stuck-on old gaskets.

4. If any exhaust studs (or holes for studs) need to be reworked, do it while the cylinder is off the engine. (If your aggravation threshold is low, pay a technician to do this kind of stuff. The fee is usually quite low.) If studs have backed out, examine their holes closely for thread damage. Retap the holes and install oversize studs if necessary. Exhaust studs come in .003, .006, .007, .009, and .012-oversize sizes.

5. Clean up the threads of all exhaust studs that are to be reused. Buy or borrow a chaser and screw it down onto each stud before proceeding with reassembly.

6. You will need a special tool of some sort to compress (and hold) the pushrod housing springs while you attempt to reinstall the housings. (The springs are quite stout.)

7. Refer to the appropriate shop manual when tightening cylinder hold-down nuts. A torque wrench is, of course, mandatory here. It's also mandatory that you follow the manufacturer's specific torquing sequence (which can be quite complex, depending on the type/model engine you have) *to the letter*. If you deviate in any way from the approved torquing recommendations, you may very well set up the kind of harmful stresses in your crankcase and/or cylinder(s) that can

later result in cracks or catastrophic failure. Read the book carefully and proceed slowly.

One more thing: If you need help, by all means consult a mechanic at once. It is easier—by far—to have a knowledgeable adviser "see you through" a difficult task than to attempt to invent a solution yourself. After all, why reinvent the wheel—or for that matter the cylinder base-nut wrench—if you don't have to?

ANOTHER WAY TO DIAGNOSE AND REMEDY STUCK RINGS

High oil consumption can mean many things: worn or scored cylinders, poor break-in, excessive crankcase pressure, or defective intake valve guides, for example. Quite often, however, it means stuck rings.

When oil usage rises due to engine *wear*, it is usually gradual. A slow rise in oil consumption over several hundred hours is normal. But ring sticking is, by contrast, usually sudden and instantaneous. The classical tipoff is a sudden *rapid* increase in oil usage—a quantum jump, unrelated to normal engine wear—along with, possibly, a loss of compression.

Question: Is there any easy way to tell if an engine has stuck rings, without pulling cylinders off? Also, can stuck rings be remedied simply and economically (i.e., without resorting to a top overhaul)? The answer to both questions is: in many cases, yes.

Criteria for Judgment

When oil cooks down to a sticky, coke-like residue and bakes your piston rings to their lands, three things happen: First, the rings no longer seat properly against the cylinder wall, because they are no longer free to expand and contract as they move up and down the cylinder; hence, blowby occurs (partially pressurizing the crankcase). Second, combustion gases cannot get behind the rings and expand them outward against the cylinder wall on the power stroke, which normally results in excess oil being wiped down to the bottom of the cylnder. Thus, extra oil passes by the rings, resulting in high oil consumption. Third, because the contour of the cylinder wall is tapered toward the top, at least when the jug is cold (a design feature referred to as "choke"), rings are rammed hard into the tapered end of the cylinder on cold startups, creating a large wear step at the top of ring travel.

When the ring grooves fill with varnish, the rings can stick. If, as shown here, they stick with their end gaps aligned, the possibilities for blowby increase tremendously.

A diagnosis of stuck rings can thus be made on the basis of [1] high crankcase pressure, [2] high oil usage, and [3] high Fe and Cr in oil analysis.

If you suspect your engine of having stuck rings, get your mechanic to attach a manometer to the crankcase breather line (being sure to seal off any vent holes in the line before proceeding; you want a pressure-tight connection). Then simply run the engine on the ground and note the crankcase pressure. According to Teledyne Continental, crankcase pressure should not exceed 4.0 inches of water with free rings on any 470- or 520-series engine. (This information is given in the test limits section of the appropriate overhaul manuals.) Lycoming does not call out crankcase pressure limits for its engines, but the upper limit of 4.0 inches would probably be valid for O-540 series engines as well.

As mentioned above, the diagnosis of stuck rings can be confirmed by a sudden dramatic increase in oil usage and by a sudden rise in iron and chromium in oil spectrum analysis. Also, cylinder compression will be down—perhaps way down, if the rings have stuck in a gaps-aligned orientation.

Preventing ring sticking is largely a matter of avoiding the use of varnish-forming oils and additives (STP is claimed by some engine experts to accelerate carbon formation inside an engine; and we have one report from a Matrix/Slick-50 user who experienced ring sticking shortly after treating his Lycoming O-320-E with the substance). It is also partly a matter of luck.

As for what can be done about it *after* it occurs, the standard procedure is to pull the cylinders off and change out the rings. A more novel (and vastly less expensive) procedure is advocated by Bill Williams, inventor of Microlon and president of the Microlon Corporation. According to Williams, rings can be unstuck by the following procedure:

1. Remove the top spark plug from the affected jug(s).

2. Bring the piston to the top of the compression stroke (feel for compression with the end of your thumb).

3. Using a funnel, pour Microlon into the spark plug boss, filling the combustion chamber completely.

4. Soak for thirty minutes.

5. Drain the remaining Microlon from the cylinder by removing the bottom spark plug and catching the fluid as it runs out.

The strong penetrants in Microlon will, says Williams, enter the ring grooves and dissolve any carbon or varnish trapped there, restoring freedom of rotation to the rings.

"Blowby in my Bellanca's IO-540 was costing me in excess of one quart per hour flying time," explains Williams. "The bottom of my airplane was covered with oil and dust after each flight. After treating my engine by this procedure, however, the blowby stopped. The airplane is clean now, and I have flown more than fifteen hours now without adding oil."

Given the fact that the above procedure relies on Microlon's penetrant power to accomplish the unsticking, rather than its Teflon content, one would think that a similar procedure employing, say, LPS-1 or WD40 (available for about $200/qt less than Microlon) would do just as well—at a much lower cost.

In either case, it is crucially important to drain *all* remaining penetrant out of the cylinder before returning the airplane to service; and it is a good idea (since the cylinder walls have been denuded of oil) to spray a light coating of engine oil inside the jugs before attempting startup.

Topside maintenance calls for sober thought and careful work imposed in part by the nature of cylinder designs and function. And that isn't the end of the story. As we shall see in the next section of this book, valves and valve lifters also pose complex problems.

Part II
VALVES

Chapter 4

VALVES AND GUIDES

It would be nice to think, after all these years of technological progress in aviation, that there are functions within aircraft engines that pilots and owners could take for granted. If there are any, valve action isn't one of them. In fact, valve problems refused to be refined away by technology, and the costs of keeping valves (and lifters) in good health have increased considerably over the 1980s.

This critical part of thrust generation can't be left untended. Consider, for instance, the salient factors that influence *valving*.

VALVE LEAD AND LAG

Valving is something pilots (and mechanics) give little thought to. Like the motion of the pistons, it's taken for granted. A valve opens, and exhaust gases are expelled; another valve opens, and intake

charge rushes in. In between, compression and combustion take place. What else is there to know?

Start with the fact that intake and exhaust valves are not equal in size (intake is bigger, because it's harder to get air to flow *in* the intake port than to get exhaust to flow *out* the exhaust port)—nor do they open and close when you expect them to.

In an idealized Otto cycle, one expects that the *exhaust valve* should open at *bottom dead center* (BDC) of piston travel, after all the energy of combustion has been extracted as mechanical work.

Likewise, you'd expect that the *intake valve* would open exactly at *top dead center* (TDC) on the intake stroke, closing again at BDC after the maximum possible quantity of intake air (and fuel) has been admitted to the cylinder. Each valve should thus be open for 80 degrees of crank travel.

Real-World Timing

Textbook illustrations of the Otto cycle are usually drawn as just described. However, a look at real-world valving reveals an entirely different picture.

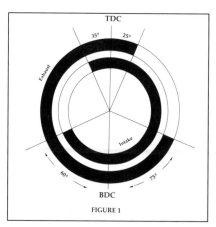

FIGURE 1

Figure 1 shows a valve-timing diagram for the Continental IO-520. (The numbers shown apply to the P/N 629726 camshaft used in all Permold-crankcase IO-520 and TSIO-520 models.) Although timing varies somewhat from one engine family to the next, the numbers shown for the IO-520 are representative of most current-production Lycoming and Continental designs.

A valve-timing diagram for the Continental IO-520. These numbers are representative of most current-production Continental and Lycoming designs. The shaded areas show the valve-open periods, the outer ring for exhaust and the inner ring for intake. The angles are crankshaft degrees from top- to bottom-dead center (TDC or BDC).

The shaded portion of the outermost ring in Figure 1 represents the "exhaust-valve open" part of the IO-520's operating cycle. (Top dead center of piston travel is at 12

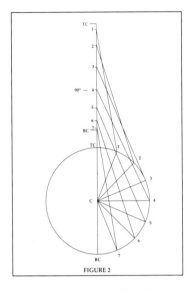

FIGURE 2

o'clock; all angles are in crankshaft degrees). Notice that—far from opening at the expected 180 degrees of crank travel—the exhaust valve actually begins opening 75 degrees before bottom center. There are several reasons for this. One is that it takes time for gases to flow out of the cylinder, and the exhaust valve doesn't open instantaneously; in fact it takes 140 degrees of crank rotation (approximately) before the valve reaches its max-lift position. For good scavenging, the valve must begin opening before BDC of piston travel.

The piston moves farther per degree of crank travel at top center than at bottom center. Notice that by the time the crank has reached 90 degrees, the piston has already traveled more than half of its total stroke.

Cylinder cooling is another reason for *valve lead*. If the exhaust valve were left closed until BDC (per the "idealized," textbook Otto cycle), a great deal of heat would be passed to the cylinder without much work being done by the piston. Careful study of piston/rod geometry (Figure 2) shows that the piston has gone through *30 percent of its total stroke* (approximately) in the first *120 degrees of crank rotation*, with the point of maximum mechanical advantage coming well before the 90-degree mark. By the time the piston has gotten to 75 degrees before BDC, most of the energy of combustion has already been extracted; what remains is mostly heat. In addition, the piston's mechanical advantage over the crankshaft is vanishingly small near BDC. There's simply no point in keeping the hot gases trapped in the cylinder after 120 degrees or so of crank rotation.

From Figure 1 it can be seen that exhaust valve *closing* does not occur until well beyond top dead center—25 degrees after TDC, in fact. This is to take advantage of gas inertia. Exhaust gases are still exiting the combustion chamber at TDC; if the valve closed then, some exhaust gases would remain trapped in the cylinder.

In summary, the exhaust valve opens at 75 degrees before BDC; it stays open the full 180 degrees of the piston's exhaust stroke; and it closes again at 25 degrees ater TDC. The total valve-open *duration* is thus 280 degrees. (Since one complete Otto cycle requires 720 degrees of crank rotation, this means that the exhaust valve is open approximately a third of the time.)

The inner ring of Figure 1 depicts intake-valve opening. Again, considerable *valve lead* and *valve lag* are evident. Instead of opening right at top center, the intake valve opens 35 degrees "ahead of schedule" to take advantage of the low pressure in the combustion chamber, which tends to suck the intake charge in. The angular distance through which both valves are open at the same time (60 degrees in this case) is called *valve overlap*. In some engines—diesels, for example—overlap can be as much as 150 degrees, to take advantage of inertia effects. (Exhaust gases, on their way out, tend to accelerate the initial inrush of intake gases.) Cylinder cooling is usually aided by valve overlap as well, but the real reason for overlap is improved *volumetric efficiency*. An engine breathes better (aspirates more air at a given manifold pressure) with some valve overlap.

Likewise, because of inertia effects, an engine draws more air if the intake valve remains open a little way past bottom dead center on the intake stroke. Remember, gases do not flow instantaneously—they require time—and the piston, when it's within 60 degrees of bottom center, does not move significantly. (In fact, because of rod geometry, it moves less—per degree of crank travel—at bottom center than at top center.) So it doesn't hurt to leave the intake valve open awhile—65 degrees, in this case—after BDC.

Once again, we see that the total valve-open duration is 280 degrees.

The Lifter Contribution

The timing values shown in Figure 1 are predicated on the use of hydraulic lifters (which maintain zero slack, or *lash*, in the valve train). Obviously, if slack were to appear between cam lobes and lifters, or lifters and pushrods, or pushrods and rocker arms, the associated valve(s) would remain closed through many more degrees of camshaft rotation, as cam lobes rose to meet the lifters and take up the slack. Timing would thus be altered. (Valves would open late and close early.) This, in turn, could significantly affect engine performance, since small changes in intake and exhaust timing can have a large effect on volumetric and thermodynamic efficiency. For example, the IO-520's effective timing with just .010-inch of lash is altered such that the total valve-open duration (intake or exhaust) is cut from 280 degrees to 230 degrees, with overlap cut from 60 degrees to 10 degrees.

In addition to making valves open late and close early, excessive lash does something else. Valve *lift* is reduced, affecting gas flow. In the IO-520, the rocker fulcrum is located so as to give a 1.33 *rocker ratio* (i.e., each millimeter of pushrod throw is converted to 1.33 mm of valve motion), so that the introduction of .010-inch of slack in the valve train converts to .067-inch less valve motion. In the IO-520, this translates to a 14-percent reduction in total lift. (The IO-520's cam lobes are .355-inch high; with 1.33 rockers, total lift is thus 0.472-inch *with zero lash.*) A lifter that bleeds down too rapidly—or collapses—can easily simulate this condition. The pilot can often detect it as a "noisy lifter" at idle. (At higher rpms, a defective lifter will usually pump up and perform nominally.)

When poor lifter action is suspected, a check should be made of "dry tappet clearance" per overhaul manual instruction. This involves bleeding the lifters down (collapsing them completely) and checking lash at the rocker toe. The factory-specified tolerance here is fairly wide (.060 to .200-inch for most engines), reflecting the wide ability of hydraulic lifters to take up valve-train slack. (See Chapter 5 for more details about lifters and their maintenance.)

The time to be most alert to valve-train mischief is immediately after overhaul. It is possible in some engines to assemble intake rockers in the exhaust position and vice-versa. It's possible in *all* engines to mis-mesh the cam and crank gears by one tooth, resulting in erratic engine operation. (On Lycomings, valve rotator caps occasionally fall off, grossly affecting lash and lift.)

Thankfully, serious valve-train problems affecting duration or lift are rare—almost as rare as the pilot who knows what "duration" and "lift" mean.

VALVES, GUIDES, AND TBO

If you have a top or major overhaul coming up, you are going to run into an ongoing parts-price horror story. Over the past decade, the price of valves has more than tripled. Furthermore, a casual inspection of a Lycoming or Continental pricelist reveals that Lycoming's valves are uniformly more expensive than Continental's—often by a factor of two. It is also immediately apparent that in every engine application (regardless of the manufacturer), exhaust valves cost several times more than intake valves. The Turbo Skylane RG's Lycoming O-540-L3C5D is a good example: The intake valve lists for no more than one-fifth the cost of the exhaust valve that sits next to it.

How Valves Differ

As it turns out, there's a good reason for the price difference between intake and exhaust valves. It has to do with the valves' operating environments. Both valves are, of course, exposed to identical combustion chamber conditions at all times. But whereas the *intake* valve is constantly cooled by an incoming flow of fuel-air mist, the *exhaust* valve is subjected, immediately after the combustion event, to a concentrated flow of hot gases approaching 1,700° Fahrenheit (or more). The blowtorch effect of the escaping exhaust hases causes an exhaust valve to run much hotter than any intake valve—so hot, in fact, that special materials and methods must be used in the exhaust valve's construction. These special materials/methods make the exhaust valve much more expensive.

The same operating factors that are responsible for the inherently short service life of mufflers and exhaust stacks (i.e.: very high

The exhaust and intake valves as seen by the piston, in this case, of a Continental O-470-R. These valves display a mild case of carbon buildup.

temperatures, extreme temperature fluctuations, exposure to atmospheres rich in carbon monoxide, ozone, lead oxide, water, etc.) are encountered in magnified form by an exhaust valve. Hence, truly extraordinary measures are called for to keep an exhaust valve in one piece. (It is not much of an exaggeration to say that an engine's TBO ulimately depends on the design of the exhaust valve.) Steels that retain sufficient strength at high temperature to be used in an exhaust valve are, unfortuantely, often too prone to corrosion to allow their use in this role. Alloys that offer good corrosion resistance, conversely, frequently can't retain their strength at high temperature. This "Catch-22" dilemma has led to two approaches in the development of reliable exhaust valves: one aimed at improving heat dissipation, and another involving the use of heat- and corrosion-resistant "superalloys" in the basic valve material. (Some valves combine the best of both approaches.)

But even using exotic materials and processes, exhaust valves—under the best of conditions—are not long-lived; both Lycoming and Continental require 100-percent replacement of exhaust (but not intake) valves at each major overhaul. Two thousand hours seems to be the upper limit on exhaust-valve life—and the majority don't even last that long.

Sodium Cooled Valves

As anyone knows, heat enters a valve via the "big end." To put it another way: Heat builds up most rapidly at the valve *face* (as you would expect), with the stem remaining somewhat cooler—due to the simple fact that the stem dissipates its heat through a much larger area than the face (i.e., through the valve guide, versus the valve seat). All other things being equal, then, anything that would serve to promote the transfer of BTUs from the valve face to the valve stem should facilitate total valve cooling.

This, in essence, is the rationale behind sodium cooling. The sodium-cooled valve—developed by Eaton for Curtiss-Wright in the 1920s—employs a hollow stem which is partially filled with elemental sodium. The sodium, a solid at less than 97.8° Celsius, melts at normal valve operating temperatures, thereafter sloshing back and forth as the valve opens and closes; heat is in this way *physically* carried from the valve face to the valve stem, where it is dissipated across the large surface area of the guide. The net result: a *cooler* valve of *more uniform overall temperature.*

Sodium-cooled exhaust valves made by Eaton Corp. are widely used in high-performance automotive, truck, and racing engines—and in Lycoming aircraft engines. (In fact, the only Lycoming exhaust valve *not* utilizing sodium cooling is the P/N 66531 valve used in the O-235-C and O-290-D.)

As you might expect, the manufacture of sodium-filled valves is no Sunday picnic. Elemental sodium spontaneously combusts on exposure to air, for example, requiring that key manufacturing steps be done in a vacuum. Altogether, some five different components are brought together in the making of a sodium-filled valve: the valve head (which is forged), the stem (spun-welded to the head in a critical process known only to a handful of the world's valve manufacturers), the sodium (injected as a powder), a specially hardened valve tip (welded to the stem), and a Stellite or Eatonite facing (puddle-welded to the valve face) for extra erosion resistance. After all these components are brought together, the valve undergoes numerous final machining, finishing, and inspection steps. How many valves are rejected in the pre-OEM stages of QC inspection is known only to Eaton, and they're not saying. "I know that at the OEM level, very, very few incoming valves are rejected," a former Big Two engineer maintains adding: "From the standpoint of quality control, exhaust valves are one of your better-made items in aviation."

Superalloy Valves

Teledyne Continental's exhaust valves, in contrast to Lycoming's, are *not* sodium-filled, which accounts for why Continental's valve prices are substantially lower than Lycoming's (an average of $100 lower across-the-board). "A decision was made very early on not to get involved in sodium valves," a retired Continental executive told *Light Plane Maintenance*. "All of Continental's valves are solid-stemmed—always have been."

Rather than opt for sodium cooling (with its attendant manufacturing problems), Continental decided to concentrate on exhaust-valve metallurgy—i.e., finding metals that, in the absence of special cooling features, can withstand high heat and corrosive atmospheres. (This has also meant paying particular attention to the choice of valve-*guide* materials—more about which shortly.) For most Continental engines, this has meant Nimonic 80A—a nickel-based "superalloy" formulation that is well known for its high-temperature strength and corrosion resistance (and for its high cost). As one engine man says, "You

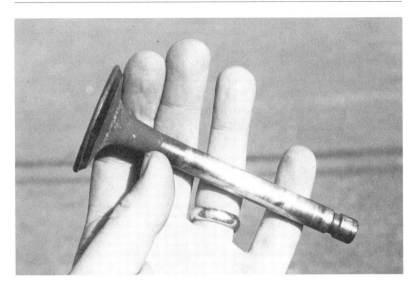

Continental's Nimonic P/N 637781 exhaust valve. This top-of-the-line nitralloy valve differs from its predecessor, the P/N 626540, in having a chrome-plated stem, for better wear characteristics. Its typical service life is 1,400 to 1,700 hours. The P/N 637781 is used in TSIO-520s but is retrofittable to other 520- and 470-series engines down to the E-185.

can either go the sodium route, which gives you valve temperatures that are low enough so that you can use cheaper, more conventional alloy materials—or you can go to a solid-stemmed valve, which is easier to make, but which runs hotter and therfore demands that you use exotic alloys. Continental chose the latter route."

Continental presently uses seven different part-number exhaust valves in its engines—all made by TRW. The price differences reflect differences in the type of materials used, and in the *quantity* of materials used. Thus, the smaller exhaust valves employed in some of the older-model Contitnental engines are forged from alloyed steels of the 21-4N and "XB" varieties, while such large valves as P/N 626540 and 637781 (for 470-series and 520-series engines) are fabricated of Nimonic 80A, an expensive nickel alloy. Some valves are chromed at the stem, others are not. Continental's most expensive valve, P/N 637781, is a chromed, Nimonic valve.

Problems with Sodium

Is the superalloy approach better than the sodium approach? "It does have its advantages, yes," our ex-Continental-engineer friend remarked. "Aside from being cheaper to make, a solid-stemmed valve is *stronger* than a hollow-stemmed valve." Is this a meaningful consideration? "I can tell you from personal experience that I have seen sodium valves from Lycoming engines that have broken in the stem area, and it's not a pretty sight. The sodium boils out all over the place. It looks like hell." Our consultant would not go so far as to characterize sodium valves as less safe than solid valves—"but they most certainly do break," he advised.

"And there's another, more subtle problem you run into when you use sodium-cooled valves," our Continental consultant explains. "For sodium cooling to work, you have to have good contact between the valve and guide, to dissipate the stem heat. Well, as an engine gets older, some clearance develops between the valve and the guide due to wear. Now what happens when you start to get a little clearance in there is that you dissipate the heat more slowly. You've broken the heat transfer path, in other words. And then, since you can't transfer the heat to the guide fast enough, the valve itself just heats up—in effect, cancelling the benefits of the sodium." At this point, our consultant explained, "you'd better be sure you have a suitable alloy material in the valve itself" (since otherwise, significant weakening could occur).

Once the heat transfer path from stem to guide is broken or altered (by excessive guide wear), the stage is set for a variety of problems. Oil which ordinarily would not find its way into the valve guide ("Valves normally run dry in their guides, for all practical purposes," our ex-Continenetal consultant points out.) *will* seep into a worn guide in modest quantities. The oil then comes into direct contact with the hot valve stem *and cooks to varnish*, creating ideal conditions for a stuck valve.

Even if a valve does not stick, excessive guide clearance can spell trouble in terms of valve seating. "If guide wear is severe enough," the ex-Continental engineer warns, "the valve will intermittently cock over slightly and seat off-center. When this happens—when one part of the valve face contacts the seat at a slight angle—a bending force can result at the stem. If the valve is already in a weakened condition— perhaps from overheating—it can, of course, then break." (Adds our consultant: "I've seen sodium-filled valves break in this fashion.")

In all fairness, it should be pointed out that solid-stemmed valves also break from time to time—but break is less apt to occur in the stem area (all other things being equal) than with hollow valves. (And no matter where they break, solid valves can't leak highly corrosive elemental sodium.)

Lycoming summed the situation up quite handily in Service Bulletin No. 293B (May 26, 1967) by saying: "It has been demonstrated that excessively worn valve guides are a distinct prelude to eventual valve failure." (On this subject, see also Service Instruction No. 1088.)

Lycoming Exhaust Valves

The trend in Lycoming exhaust valve design for the past 20 years has been toward thicker stems, introduction of sodium cooling for smaller and smaller engines, and the use of more advanced alloys in sodium valves.

A total of six types of exhaust valves are now used in Lycoming engines:

1. Solid-stemmed valves (as mentioned earlier) are still used in certain O-235 and O-290 engines, although sodium-cooled replacements are available (and recommended, in view of their better erosion characteristics with high-lead fuel).

2. 7/16-inch diameter-stem sodium-cooled valves are specified in certain VO-360 models for helicopter use. At one time, of course, 7/16-inch vlaves were used in the majority of Lycoming engines. But in 1966, Lycoming began phasing out those valves in lieu of the thicker-stemmed, more reliable 1/2-inch valves that are now used.

3. Half-inch sodium-cooled valves are employed in a variety of Lycoming engines (one size valve fits several different engine families).

4. Chrome-plated 1/2-inch sodium valves are used in a variety of 320-, 360-, and 540-series Lycomings.

5. Inconel 1/2-inch sodium-cooled valves, P/N 76081, are used in several O-540 models, plus the IO-320-C (Twin Comanche) and the TO-360-E1A6D (Turbo Seminole).

6. Nimonic 1/2-inch sodium-filled valves are employed in Lycoming's brawniest engines, the TIGO-541s of Pressurized Navajo fame.

Of all these types, Lycoming's Inconel valves represent perhaps the state of the art in piston-engine valve manufacture, combining the best of two worlds: sodium cooling and superalloy strength. Inconel, like Nimonic 80A, is a tremendously heat-strong, corrosion-resistant nickel-chromium-titanium alloy, containing trace amounts of manganese, carbon, cobalt, silicon, aluminum, tantalum, and columbium.

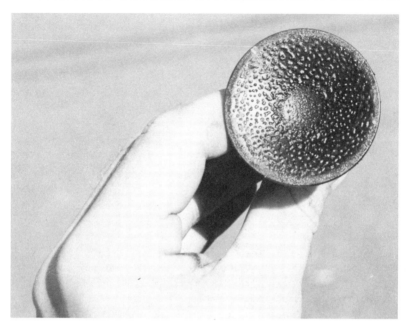

The severe varnish buildup on this Lycoming exhaust valve is typical of a cylinder that is using excessive oil.

(Nimonic 80A is similarly exotic but contains five-percent iron, whereas iron is absent from Inconel.) The use of Inconel in a sodium-cooled exhaust valve thus affords the ultimate in high-temperature reliability—and in cost.

How do you know which valve combinations are approved for your engine? The Parts Manual for your engine contains this information. With Lycoming engines, however, you should also cross-check the most recent edition of Service Instruction No. 1037. S.I. 1037 gives approved valve—and piston and ring—combinations for all Lycoming engines, and it's generally more up-to-date than most Parts Manuals.

How to Extend Valve Life

There are many approaches to saving money on valves. One is to buy new parts only from discount PMA (Parts Manufacturer Approvals, granted by the FAA) sources. The other approach: make your present valves last longer—which means (among other things) not replacing valves unnecessarily. Many shops, to reduce after-sale service problems, prefer to retire all exhaust valves (on a knee-jerk basis) automatically in the course of a top overhaul, rather than put existing valves back in service. This may be a profitable policy for shops, but it is needlessly profligate from the plane-owner's standpoint. As long as a valve (any valve) meets Table of Limts specs (as spelled out in the appropriate manufacturer's *Overhaul Manual*), it can—and should—be kept in service.

As for prolonging a valve's life, there are several things a pilot/owner can do. One is to fly frequently (which helps reduce corrosion and gum buildup), and change oil and filters often. Poor oil/filter maintenance is a factor in valve guide wear, tappet wear, and sludge buildup—all of which are bad for valves, one way or another.

Valve-train wear can also be minimized through the use of Lycoming LW16702 oil additive (one can per oil change), which contains a

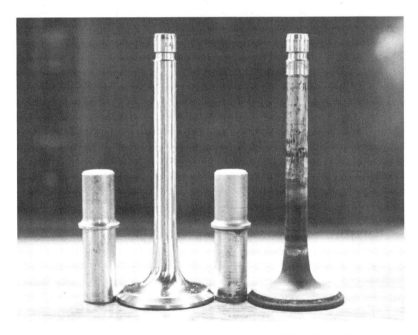

Continental's nitralloy valve guides come prefinished from the factory, so there is no need for final reaming in the field, and they are nitride-hardened on the inside diameter. Hard rubbing of the valve stem against the guide I.D. can cause severe erosion, as shown here on the right. The valve on the left is new.

proven automotive anti-scuff agent. Microlon may also be of some benefit, although hard data is lacking on this score.

One of the more important things you can do to keep your valves happy is to reduce your engine's lead intake. If you can do so, switch to 100L from 100 "green"; to 80-octane from 100LL; and to unleaded automotive gasoline from 80-octane. (Do not, in any case, however, operate on a fuel that is lower in octane number than the minimum specified for your engine.) Many people in the industry believe that the rise in valve-related problems in general aviation over the past ten years is directly attributable to the growing use of high-lead fuels, and the disappearance of 80-octane. (You'll recall that 80-octane avgas contains one-fourth the tetraethyl lead of 100LL, and less than *one eighth* that of "green" 100-octane.) The recent proliferation of service bulletins pertaining to lead problems and valves certainly supports this view. Our own opinion, having examined valves from high-lead-burning engines as well as from engines that have seen only low-lead gasoline, is that lead spells death for exhaust valves, not only in terms of deposits on the valve face, but erosion and pitting around the neck of the valve. Consequently, anything that tends to remove lead from an engine, in our opinion, can only have a salutary effect on valve life.

In general, anything you can do to [1] keep your oil clean, [2] keep excess lead out of your engine, and [3] reduce cylinder operating temperatures will have a life-prolonging effect on your exhaust valves.

Valve Guides and Valve Wear

Valve *guide* wear is tied intimately to valve longevity. As mentioned above, rapid or erratic wear of a valve guide can set in motion a self-aggravating circle of destructive events, starting with the breaking of the heat transfer path from valve to cylinder head, and leading to valve overheating, more rapid guide (and valve) wear, more overheating, more wear, etc.—which increases the likelihood of valve sticking, valve breakage, valve erosion, preignition, loss of compression, and/or a top overhaul.

As Lycoming's service department pointed out in Service Bulletin No. 293B (May 1967): "It has been demonstrated that excessively worn valve guides *are a distinct prelude to eventual valve failure.*"

In attempting to reduce guide wear to a minimum, aircraft engine manufacturers have tried various valve guide materials over the years, starting with babbitt-bronze and progressing to aluminum-bronze, cast iron (or ni-resist), and finally—in the case of Continental engines—nitride-hardened steel alloy (or nitralloy).

Continental, in particular, has paid close attention to the selection of guide materials, since its engines all use solid exhaust valves, which run hotter than Lycoming's sodium-cooled counterparts. The nitralloy guides that are used in Continental's largest engines (retrofittable to E-series, O-470, and IO-470 engines as well) are significantly more expensive than the cast-iron and aluminum-bronze guides they replaced, although some of that expense is due to the nitralloy guides' being prehoned to final I.D. at the factory, and the nitralloy guides are sufficiently hardened that only chrome-plated valves can be used with them. (Note: Continental has also gone to extra-thick chrome-plating of its big-valve stems, to further address the stem/guide wear issue. The thick-chrome valves are Superior P/N 643873.)

For optimum valve and guide life in a 470-or-larger series Continental engine, Continental has also recommended using nitralloy guides (P/N 641951), P/N 637881 or equivalent exhaust valves, high-flow tappets (P/N 641709) in the exhaust position (to get more cooling oil to the valve stem). (See Service Bulletin M82-6.) The ultimate objectives were longer and TBOs.

Almost as soon as they were introduced, however, nitralloy guides began giving trouble. Some operators noted that the guides were cutting into valve stems, sending tiny shavings of chrome to he oil filter. Early reports of trouble were ultimately blamed on faulty manufacture of the guides (specifically, the presence of a sharp lip on the I.D. of the guide, leftover from machining at the factory).

Recent reports indicate, however, that even when guides are properly deburred and radiused, valve stem erosion (from direct metal/metal contact) is still possible with nitralloy.

The message to owners of large Continental engines now seems to be: Keep an eye on valve-to-guide clearance (which can be checked easily at 100-hour inspections), and if clearances are opening up dramatically—i.e., a back-and-forth wobble of .005- or .010-inch—be ready to face top overhaul. (And at that time, consider going back to ni-resist valve guides.)

The *real* cure could turn out to be roller-tipped rocker arms. Existing rockers exert considerable side-load on the valve stem during normal valve opening. This side-pressure is eliminated with roller-tipped rockers.

Lycoming does not offer a nitralloy valve guide—nor, strictly speaking, is one called for, given Lycoming's use of sodium-cooled valves. Lycoming's best valve guides (P/N 75838, P/N 74230) are thus ni-resist cast iron. Like Continental's ni-resist guides, these guides are rough-finished on the inside diameter and must be final-reamed to the appropriate I.D. by the installing mechanic.

Is there any way to increase the service life of Lycoming valve guides (besides using ni-resist wherever possible)? As a matter of fact, yes. Lycoming has found that the surface finish of the inside diameter of the valve guide is critical in determining the wear characteristics of the valve and guide. Rather than ream guides to final I.D. per *Overhaul Manual* instructions, Lycoming is now recommending that mechanics *hone* (or rough-ream and *then* hone) the guide to the final specified I.D. leaving a 30-micro-inch RMS surface finish.

According to Lycoming Service instruction No. 1200A, dated October 1, 1982, "It has been found that many operators are failing to achieve the specified surface finish when reaming valve guide I.D. and consequently, accelerated wear is occuring between the valve stem and valve guide." Furthermore: "Service experience has shown that if the valve guide is honed to specified dimensions, the desired smoothness and resultant better wear may be obtained."

We see no reason why the 30-micro-inch surface hone should not prove beneficial to Continental engine owners (with ni-resist guides), too. Have your mechanic look into this the next time your guides are replaced.

On-the-Aircraft Checks

One might ask whether there's anything the pilot can do *between* overhauls to keep tabs on valve health (aside from performing a compression test at each annual). When we put this question to our engine consultant, a Continental engineer of some 27 years' experience, he offered the following words of advice:

"The first thing a plane owner can do is every once in a while look inside the cylinders with a borescope. This will tell you whether you've got bad erosion problems at the valve face.

"Second thing you can do is drop the exhaust risers down and shine a flashlight into your cylinders' exhaust ports. You can see the *back* side of the valve face this way, quite easily. Look for pitting, erosion. You'd be surprised what you can see back in there sometimes. I've looked in there on some engines and seen stems that were eroded to half their original thickness. Scares the life out of you! Any engine that's burning high-lead fuel, you should take a look inside the exhaust ports every few hundred hours, at least.

"Third, do a 'wobble test' on your valves now and then, to detect guide wear. Lycoming has a Service Instruction on this, I think." (It's S.I. 1088.) "Basically, you just take the rocker covers off the cylinders and reach in there with a screwdriver or something and try to wiggle your valves back and forth in their guides. Lycoming has a whole big procedure, with feeler gages and whatnot—that's a little silly, if you ask me. You don't need all that. The important thing is to compare one valve to another, and if you find a loose one, think seriously about replacing it."

How loose is loose?

"Well, that's something you just have to get a feel for. Obviously, you expect to have a few thousandths' clearance. Lycoming, I think, says forty thousandths [of an inch] is the maximum sideplay. I think if I saw twenty thousandths on my engine, I'd be concerned."

How often?

"I'd do a wobble test every 500 hours or so." (Lycoming recommends the procedure at the half-TBO mark.)

No valve lasts forever, obviously; but if you'll be good to your valves, chances are they'll (ahem) "reciprocate."

VALVE STICKING

Valve sticking episodes have been on the rise of late. In fact, this trend apparently goaded Lycoming into issuing a service letter (dated July 2, 1982; S.L. No. L197) devoted entirely to this subject. A great many complaints have involved Lycoming O-320-H2AD, O-320-D2J/D3J, O-540-L3C5D and -J3C5D powerplants, but all engines are vulnerable to valve sticking, a malady that can be frightening and lethal.

"One of our own 172s had a bout with it," the chief mechanic of a large northeastern Cessna dealer reports. "A customer came back from a rental flight in the plane and said, 'Gee, this thing sure runs rough when you first start it up.' I immediately took the plane off the rental line. Next morning, I started it up myself—and the customer was right, it ran rough as a cob. After shutting it down, I made a quick check and the number-two cylinder was stone-cold. That was a dead give-away. I knew right then we had an intermittent sticking valve in that jug. We were lucky to catch it at an early stage."

Not everyone is so lucky. One member of a flying club recalls a harrowing experience in a late-model Skyhawk: "We were on a cross-country, with four of us on board. One minute, the engine was running fine—the next minute, wham! It was vibrating like you wouldn't believe. I immediately enrichened the mixture and reduced power, and looked for an airport. Luckily, we made it down okay, but it had us shook up quite a bit. When the mechanic looked under the cowl, there were two pushrod tubes bent out of shape—two valves had stuck."

The scenario could have been even worse. Depending on how far open or closed a valve is when it sticks, irreparable damage can occur not only to valves, guides, and pushrods, but lifters, cams, and pistons. (A wide-open valve can contact the piston in almost any high-compression engine.) And a holed piston often means metal throughout the motor.

An Old Problem

Valve sticking in small Lycomings is nothing new, as it turns out. In 1943, when U.S. Army liaison aircraft powered by Lycoming O-435-1 engines—certified on low-lead (1.0 ml TEL/gal) 73-octane avgas—were forced to switch to high-lead (3.0 ml TEL/gal) 80-octane "all purpose" motor fuel, valve sticking became common, if not rampant. (The same problem existed in O-290 ground-power units, which used identical cylinder assemblies to the O-435.)

As a direct result of poor experience with liaison aircraft in combat zones, Lycoming—aided by the Ethyl Research Laboratories and the U.S. Army—undertook substantial testing to determine which valve/guide combinations were most resistant to sticking, erosion, burning, etc., with additional tests to investigate the roles of fuel and oil. The tests (which continued even after the war) were far from conclusive, unfortunately. They did show, however, that:

1. Incomplete burning of fuels plays a role in deposit formation.

2. Deposits formed on the "neck" of the valve (i.e., the area behind the face, exposed to hot gases in the exhaust port) are important in some instances of valve sticking, since the accumulation of excessive material here can physically prevent the valve from retracting into the guide.

3. The degree of guide lubrication plays a role in episodes of sticking, particularly in sodium-valve engines (which all production Lycoming engines now are). As Robert V. Kerley of the Ethyl Corporation explained in a paper in *SAE Quarterly Transactions*, Vol. 1, No.

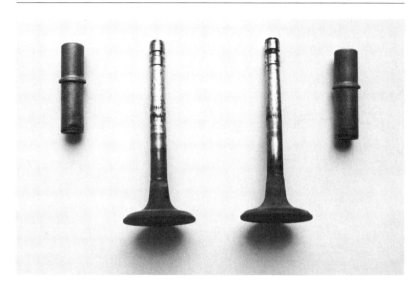

Valve sticking often occurs when deposits accumulate on the stem area behind the valve face, hindering retraction of the valve into the guide. Shown here are two Continental IO-520 exhaust valves and their respective guides.

2 (April 1947): "Practice has indicated that sodium-cooled valves will tend to increase valve-sticking troubles unless lubrication is increased, preferably by an oil jet to the stem, or unless the stem is run dry. Light or moderate lubrication normally causes coke formation resulting in sticking." (Today, when a Lycoming engine is delivered new, the exhaust valve to guide clearance is typically only .003-inch— and the stem essentially runs dry. With 500 to 600 hours of wear, the clearance opens up, and oil enters the guide. This seems to be when the trouble starts.)

4. Valve guide length is an important consideration. *Shorter*-than-usual guides must be used with sodium-filled valves, to avoid sticking, since any protrusion of the bottom of the guide beyond the exhaust port wall tends to encourage deposit buildup.

5. Valve rotators are of limited help in preventing sticking.

6. Dust and impurities carried by the oil play a role in deposit buildup on valves (which precedes sticking, generally).

Valve sticking can be of two types. Hot sticking occurs while the engine is in operation. The engine runs smoothly one minute, then very rough the next; often, more than one valve sticks, and frequently there's pushrod damage. *Cold* sticking, on the other hand, occurs after shutdown or during periods of inactivity. The pilot's first indication of trouble is on startup: the engine catches, but runs poorly, and only smooths out after it has had a few minutes to warm up. This is what many A&Ps refer to fondly as "morning sickness."

Even today, nearly 40 years after Lycoming's (and Ethyl Labs') landmark tests, valve sticking is a poorly understood phenomenon. Hot sticking seems to be associated with *guide* deposits (perhaps, though not necessarily, resulting from entry of oil into the guide on the rocker arm side), while cold sticking can be due either to guide deposits or mechanical hindrance from deposits on the neck area of the valve. (In its early stages, the latter process produces incomplete seating of the valve under static conditions, giving rise to poor compression on a differential compression test.) According to William A. Gruse, writing in *Motor Oils* (Reinhold, 1967), under-head deposits of the latter kind "are likely to be high in lead compounds and other organic solids—metal and dust." (Hence the need for adequate filter maintenance.) "The underhead material will disturb the heat flow involved in cooling the valve. When it accumulates sufficiently, it may wear the end of the guide to a bell-mouthed condition." (This is, in fact, often observed in aircraft guides after several hundred hours.) "This could cause the valve to fall eccentrically into the valve seat and, in effect, to hang open."

What's more, since incomplete combustion is thought to aggravate the deposit buildup that precedes valve ticking, it's interesting to note (as Gruse does in his book) that a poorly seated valve may—by allowing leakage—encourage further poor combustion, leading to more deposits, poorer combustion, and so on.

The Role of Fuel and Oil

Anyone who would understand valve sticking would do well to pay attention to the work of William Gruse. A former member of ASTM and SAE committees on motor fuels and oils, Dr. Gruse is a world-renowned authority on fuels and lubricants. As one reviewer states, "His earlier studies on...the effective analysis of exhaust valve sticking alone is sufficient to establish his international reputation."

As far as valve sticking goes, Gruse established early on that varnish formation was important; and here, the composition of fuel played a major role. "Use of radioactive elements as tracers," reports Gruse, "has supported the idea that aromatics and aromatic olefins are major

The Turbo Skylane's Lycoming O-540-L3C5D appears to have a high incidence of stuck-valve episodes, as large engines go. In general, sodium-valve engines such as this are more prone to valve sticking than are engines with solid-stemmed exhaust valves.

offenders, simple olefins less so, and paraffins the least serious." The aromatic content of avgas *and* autogas in recent years has risen dramatically (in fact, 100LL contains up to 25 percent aromatics). Perhaps not coincidentally, so has the rate of valve sticking.

Oil plays a role, too. Apparently, lead (from leaded gasoline) and incompletely oxidized fuel byproducts (from blowby) can be carried to distant hot spots in the engine by circulating oil—ultimately causing varnish formation. In one particularly ingenious experiment, Gruse rigged a V-type two-cylinder test engine with two carburetors (one for each jug) in such a way as to feed non-varnishing fuel to one cylinder but varnish-promoting fuel to the other cylinder. He found that after 40 hours, the engine accumulated varnish in equal amounts *in both cylinders.*

"The crankcase oil furnished the only plausible medium by which varnish material formed in one cylinder could reach the other," wrote Gruse. (This experiment was repeated many times, in various ways. When the oil was changed every hour, varnish did not accumulate in either cylinder after 40 hours—confirming Gruse's conclusion that the oil helps carry varnish precursors throughout the engine.)

The advent of high-dispersancy oils has done a lot to alleviate varnishing in modern engines; but even so, there is a limit to what oil can do, particularly if operating conditions favor moisture buildup. (High blowby and/or infrequent operation are instrumental here.) As Dr. Gruse sums up: "The mixture of partly oxidized gasoline or diesel fuel already reacted with nitrogen oxides, together with oil oxidized by high-temperature contact with air and peroxides, the whole mixed with water, forms an excellent promoter of varnish formation."

Inactivity, chronic low-power operation, the use of unstable or aged fuels, high blowby, overrich or overlean operation, infrequent oil changes, and inattention to filters, all point the way to valve and piston varnish—and ultimately, valve sticking.

Prevention

So much for etiology. What, if anything, can be done to *prevent* valve deposits and sticking?

Lycoming's service letter on this subject (No. L197) starts by acknowledging the importance of clean fuel and oil, and insinuates that owners are not paying as much attention to regular oil/filter changes as they should. (We tend to agree. Unless oil analysis tells you otherwise, drain the garbage out of your crankcase every 25 to 50 hours. Oil-change intervals of more than 50 hours spell trouble in all but a very few special circumstances.)

But dispensing with the obvious. Lycoming's letter does go on to much more serious advice: "If the aircraft is not flown regularly, the risk of valve sticking is increased due to the buildup of moisture, acids, gums, and lead sludge in the oil," says S.L. L197, adding: "Infrequent periods of ground running that do not allow the engine to reach operating temperature can *also contribute to valve sticking...* [During ground running] the engine operates on a richer mixture than when flying. During flight at cruise power, the mixture is normally leaned and much of its lead content vaporizes. Ideally, the engine should be leaned to peak EGT at cruise power settings. This produces optimum combustion and lessens contaminant buildup."

Also: "Exposing the engine to rapid cool down, as when losing altitude suddenly with the power reduced, can also cause valve sticking. Rapid cool down can occur on the ground as well, if the engine is shut off too soon after landing. The engine should have *at least five minutes of slow running or idling time immediately after landing to moderate cool-down temperatures."*

Al Hundere, of Alcor, Inc. (makers of TCP Concentrate), has another recommendation: use TCP. "The deposits formed on valves when TCP is used are softer in texture and therefore less likely to hang the valve in the guide. I've never seen valve sticking in any engine where TCP has been used regularly."

Still another tip: If oil coking or varnish are suspected, switch to a non-coking oil. That means a synthetic. Shell Multigrade 15W-50 (which is partially synthetic) is a step in the right direction. If you can afford them, the true synthetics—such as Amsoil's "Avoil," or Bel-Ray Aero 1—are probably better, since coking, varnishing, and oxidation are virtually unknown when operating with synthetic oils.

Clean Combustion

Perhaps the key to avoiding valve sticking is good (i.e., thorough) combustion.

When a hydrocarbon fuel is completely burned, combustion results in the formation of water and carbon dioxide only. In an Otto-cycle engine, in the real world, perfect combustion is rarely attainable, since it requires a perfect ratio of fuel to air (with neither in excess) in all cylinders—and even then, it requires special fuels. An engine fed pure methane can approach complete combustion; but a Continental or Lycoming engine fed gasoline (a complex "soup" of over 100 different molecular species) cannot. There will always be some byproducts of incomplete combustion in a conventional aircraft engine.

But you *can* control combustion byproducts to a great degree, by [1] proper use of the mixture control, [2] regular attention to spark plug maintenance, and [3] use of low-lead fuels and/or TCP (to discourage harmful lead products). All of these are interrelated.

Why are spark plugs important? Simply because misfiring contributes to poor combustion. (On a dual-ignition engine, spark timing is set so as to take advantage of the complete combustion afforded by a dual flame front. The fouling of one spark plug in a two-plug cylinder can and does affect the "completeness" of combustion.) This fact was noted in Embry-Riddle Aeronautical University's TCP trials of seven years ago. "Shortly after the ERAU fleet began operating with 100LL," the University report states, "spark plug fouling incidents rose tenfold and valve sticking problems increased from one per 7,500 flight hours to one in every 2,000 hours." Further: "The [TCP] test was based on the premise that the highly leaded 100LL fuel was causing excessive spark plug misfiring. This misfiring resulted in unacceptable byproducts. The byproducts, circulating in the oil, caused the valve sticking....There is evidence to indicate a reduction in valve sticking may be expected."

Oil Fortification

Many aircraft owners—and no small number of IAs and A&Ps—say that valve sticking can also be averted through regular use of Marvel Mystery Oil, an automotive oil and fuel additive widely available through department stores, auto parts stores, etc.

"Back in the DC-2 days, we used to use Marvel Mystery Oil by the 55-gallon drum," a retired Braniff captain told *Light Plane Maintenance*. "Without it, we'd have had stuck valves in every plane, on every route." Marvel oil lacks FAA approval, acceptance, or acknowledgement of any type. "I believe CAA knew what we were doing back in the thirties and forties, however," says the retired captain (who now uses Marvel oil in his Cessna 172).

Many A&Ps apparently agree. "My brother used to have a garage," an A&P with a large Cessna dealership told us. "We used to put Marvel in everything. Every once in a while, a customer would pull up in some heap, and the valves would be hammering real loud. We'd leave the engine running and pour some Marvel oil in. The *clacketa-clacketa-clacketa* would slowly go away—clacket-mmmm-clack-mmmmmm—while we were standing there, in a matter of seconds. Pretty soon the valve noise was gone completely. It was amazing. If I had a plane myself, I'd use it, no question about it."

We're not in a position to recommend that owners go out and try Marvel Mystery Oil (or any unapproved product) in an airplane. (Frankly, we wouldn't use it in the fuel, since it's almost certain to reduce the octane rating.) But many owners and mechanics swear by the product as an aid to preventing—even curing—valve sticking.

We just thought we'd mention it.

Worst Case

What do you do if your engine begins to show telltale signs of valve sticking (i.e., "morning sickness" type roughness that smooths out as the engine warms up, accompanied by one or more cold cylinders)?

Fortunately, there's an easy trick that can save you a top overhaul, in some instances. It involves reaming the valve guides with the cylinder in place.

"What you do," an experienced Cessna mechanic told us, "is this. First you take the rocker cover off, remove the rockers and valve springs, and push the valve down into the cylinder with the piston at bottom-dead-center. If the valve is stuck, you can unstick it by feeding rope into one spark plug hole—feed as much as you can fit in there—then turning the prop so that the piston comes back up and presses hard on the rope and, also, the valve. It helps to have the valve springs still installed if you do this, because at some point the valve will free up and the springs will cause it to snap closed with a loud 'clank'.

"Anyway, all you do is drop the valve down into the cylinder, move it out of the way by manipulating it with mechanical fingers through a spark plug hole, and ream the valve guide just enough to remove any deposits in it. You can look at the valve stem by pulling it up through a spark plug hole. If the stem is obviously defective, you'll want to pull the jug and replace the valve, and do a top. If not, you can polish it with crocus cloth or whatever. Ream the guide in accordance with Lycoming Service Instruction 1200A. Then check its I.D. per the overhaul manual Table of Limits. Reassemble the valve, walnut-blast the cylinder to remove deposits, and you're done."

Many mechanics will insist on a top overhaul rather than trying the above procedure, protesting that an exhaust valve guide—reamed in this manner—will fall outside the acceptable inner-diameter limits, particularly if it has many hundreds of hours in service.

T'ain't necessarily so. Point out the paragraph in Lycoming's Table of Limits (Publication SSP2070-3, page 7) that says that engines having half-inch valves "may have exhaust valve guides that are .003 in. over the maximum inside diameter limit, anytime up to 300 hours in service." Furthermore: "After 300 hours service, inside diameter of exhaust valve guide may increase *.001 in. during each 100 hours of operation up to the recommended overhaul time for the engine.*" (Emphasis added.)

A word to the wise: If your engine experiences what you feel may be a bout with intermittent valve sticking, check your pushrod tubes prior to the next flight. Any unsightly bends or bulges mean (obviously) that the engine should be grounded until further investigation can be made.

"We had a call a few weeks ago from the owner of a Skylane RG," the chief mechanic for a large Cessna dealer recalls. "From the symptoms he was telling us, it sounded like he had had what we call 'morning sickness'. I sent one of our guys out—this was at a field some 30 miles away—expecting maybe we could have the guy flying again in short order. Well, when the cowling came off, there was one bent pushrod housing and two stuck valves. What's more, *all* the exhaust valves had to be driven out—the varnish was that bad. The plane had only 700 or 800 hours."

Our favorite Cessna mechanic furthermore states that he is occasionally finding broken lifter bodies in engines that have hung valves—a serious form of damage requiring that the crankcase be split for repair. (Continental lifters can be removed without splitting the case.)

What's more, when the problem occurs in Cessna 172s (1976 and later), it seems to affect the number-two cylinder more often than not. "I don't know why that should be," our man reports.

As said before, valve sticking can happen to any type of engine. But operators of small Lycomings (O-320s and low-hp O-540s) should be especially vigilant. Prevention, as always, is the best cure.

Chapter 5

HYDRAULIC VALVE LIFTERS

As we saw in chapter 4, hydraulic valve lifters (often called *hydraulic tappets*) can make trouble. The problems can manifest themselves in mysterious ways—a simple and seasonal loss of top-end power, or differences in engine acceleration rates on takeoff in a twin, or a marked split in manifold pressures, or a regular miss or vibration at high power that actually *subsides* at low power. These are signs that call for attention. In this chapter, we will dig deeper into lifters (again, at the risk of some necessary repetition) to examine their nature, vulnerabilities and questions of maintenance.

FEATURES, FUNCTIONS, AND FAULTS

Hydraulic lifters, or tappets, come in a variety of sizes and styles, but all are designed to do the same thing: Eliminate valve lash. Without plunger-action hydraulic lifters to "take up slack" in the valve train, large clearances would exist between cam lobe and valve

stem in a pushrod-type engine, due to the thermal expansion of parts at normal operating temperatures. Cam lobes would mercilessly (and noisily) slap valves open instead of *smoothly* pressing them open, and component lives would suffer. Also, of course, valve timing would vary with engine temperature—a distinctly unsatisfactory situation.

Hydraulic tappets have certain features, regardless of model or design. All have a spring-loaded plunger (against which the pushrod presses) riding inside a bored-out lifter *body* with oil holes in the sides and a check valve (disc-type or ball-type; both are used) to keep the body full of oil for each leak-down cycle. The key thing to note is that the "slack" in the valve train is taken up by oil (not by spring pressure), and the tappet is self-adjusting in length. Also, since the tappet is a kind of viscous damper, the leakdown rate of the plunger in the bore is of paramount importance.

The tappet, you'll notice, is also a key part of the engine lubrication circuit: Oil must pass the tappet to get to the rocker box. (Oil flows through the hollow pushrods to arrive at rocker bearings and associated squirt jets aimed at the valve stems. Gravity action returns runoff to the sump via special rocker drainback tubes in Lycoming engines, or via the pushrod housings themselves in a Continental.) Depending on various features of tappet design, lifters can send oil "upstairs" at a high flow rate or a low flow rate.

Same and different

Intake and exhaust tappets are the same, but once they are removed from their bores, they should not be intermixed (unless a new cam and new—or reconditioned—lifters are to be put in service).

Continental and Lycoming lifters are easy to tell apart—usually. Teledyne favors the automotive-style "barrel type" lifter for almost all of its engines, whereas Lycoming uses the mushroom-type lifter (with a tuliped head or face riding against the cam) for most applications. But there are notable exceptions. Lycoming tried using barrel-type lifters in the O-320-H and O-360-E, with less than perfect success. Continental, conversely, used mushroom lifters in many of its early designs, including the A-65 and E-185.

Is one type preferable to the other? Not really. But an important point in Continental's favor (and in favor of the Lycoming O-320-H and O-360-E, for what it's worth) is that barrel-type tappets are easy to remove from an engine in the middle of a TBO run (if, for example, you want to check the condition of your cam lobes without tearing the

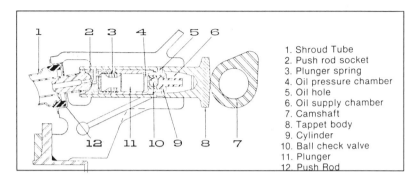

1. Shroud Tube
2. Push rod socket
3. Plunger spring
4. Oil pressure chamber
5. Oil hole
6. Oil supply chamber
7. Camshaft
8. Tappet body
9. Cylinder
10. Ball check valve
11. Plunger
12. Push Rod

Mushroom-style valve lifter, or tappet (Lycoming).

engine down). By contrast, mushroom-style tappets, because the big end rides against the cam (inside a crankcase bore that is much narrower than the tulip), *can't be removed without splitting the crankcase.*

Little-Known Facts

Hydraulic lifters are the most precisely-made parts in your engine. The plunger and body of a lifter are electronically classified to 33 millionths of an inch and hand-assembled in matched grades to provide two to three ten-thousandths' clearance between plunger O.D. and body I.D. The outside diameter of the lifter body is held to tolerances of about five ten-thousandths (.0005) of an inch to assure a proper fit in the crankcase bore. The lifter foot or face is polished to six micro-inches, specially hardened, and 100-percent Rockwell tested for hardness. (If you see tiny fly-speck-like dimples on the face of a lifter, that's not pitting; those are the Rockwell marks.)

The face of a lifter is rounded—it is not ground perfectly flat, but has a radius of about 30 inches. This curvature, combined with the slant or taper of the cam lobe (a couple thousandths' or so per inch of width) ensures that the tappet contact area is displaced to one side; and this, in turn, ensures that the tappet *rotates* in service.

Of course, rotating tappets tend to cause their crankcase bores to wear egg-shaped. If this egg-shaped profile is not restored to cylindrical during the overhaul of the engine, at some point the tappets will stop rotating in service—and spalling (or other problems) will begin.

Depending on valve spring pressure and other parameters, the localized peak loads seen at the cam lobe and tappet face can be as high as 150,000 psi in normal service, which effectively squeezes the oil film

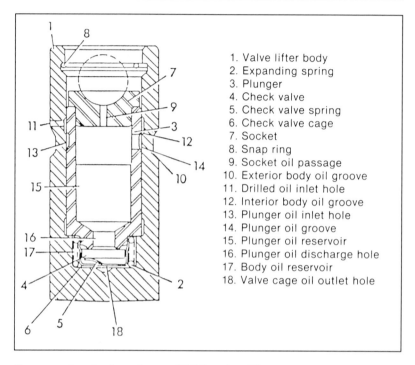

1. Valve lifter body
2. Expanding spring
3. Plunger
4. Check valve
5. Check valve spring
6. Check valve cage
7. Socket
8. Snap ring
9. Socket oil passage
10. Exterior body oil groove
11. Drilled oil inlet hole
12. Interior body oil groove
13. Plunger oil inlet hole
14. Plunger oil groove
15. Plunger oil reservoir
16. Plunger oil discharge hole
17. Body oil reservoir
18. Valve cage oil outlet hole

Components of a barrel-type (TCM) valve lifter.

on the moving parts to but a few molecules thick. In this localized high-psi high-friction zone, the oil reaches so-called flash temperatures of up to 400° Fahrenheit. This puts interesting demands on an engine's lubricating oil.

Obviously, the slightest introduction of dirt to a hydraulic lifter, either inside the bore or at the face, can lead to Big Problems in a Hurry in terms of face scuffing and/or plunger sticking. The bigger problem, interestingly, is not the former but the latter. While it's true that the smallest grain of dirt can breach the oil film at the cam lobe face and cause metal gouging (indeed, this happens often), the tiny gouges, generally speaking, quickly "heal over." A small buildup of dirt or varnish in the tappet body, however, can easily cause a plunger to stick in the collapsed position. And then you have valve hammering, and/or valve burning.

A clue to the seriousness of invading dirt or sludge is provided by Paragraph 6-29 of the Continental O-470/IO-470 *Overhaul Manual*: "If a hydraulic tappet will not maintain zero lash in the valve train, its plunger may be held inward by ring of carbon or scored by abrasive particles in the oil, or the check valve may be held open by a sludge deposit. Any such condition should be brought to the *operator's attention*, since it *indicates a need for more frequent inspection and cleaning of the oil filter."*

Dry Tappet Clearance

For smooth valve operation to occur, an engine's *dry tappet clearance* must be within limits (i.e., with the tappets fully collapsed, there must not be excessive clearance between the valve train components), and the tappets themselves must, of course, provide proper damping action.

Dry tappet clearance is something that is not often checked except at overhaul time, and sometimes not even then. The procedures—and the appropriate "go/no-go" limits—are spelled out in detail in the Overhaul Manual for your engine. Basically, to make the measurement, you simply remove the valve covers from the cylinders you intend to check; turn the prop until both valves are fully seated on the

Hydraulic tappets vary in design, but they all perform the same basic function of eliminating valve-train lash. Shown here is a typical Continental tappet, one from an IO-470-N, disassembled into its component parts: barrel (top), spring (right), plunger and check valve, socket and socket retaining clip. The plunger is held in the body by a snap-ring. The oil hole in the side of the barrel admits engine oil from the crankcase galleries. This type of tappet is easily removed between TBOs.

compression stroke; use a special prybar or tool to compress the hydraulic lifter for one or the other valve; then insert a feeler between the valve tip and rocker face. (For most Lycoming engines, the allowable limits are .028-inch to .080-inch; for the big Continentals, it's .060-inch to .200-inch.) If dry tappet clearance falls outside the prescribed limits, the situation must be corrected by installing shorter or longer pushrods.

Bad things happen when dry tappet clearance goes awry (as, for instance, when excessive wear occurs at the cam, the rod ends, or the rocker arm). Too-small clearances can result in burned valves or poor compression, while too-large clearances can result in valve hammering and engine roughness.

Even more critical for valve longevity is proper tappet *damping action*. When damping action is lost, valve-train componentas smack into each other with all the subtlety of a jackhammer pounding a piece of pavement. Valves do not take kindly to such treatment. In fact, the violent hammering of valves against seats that occurs when tappets "lunch out" has been known to result in the sudden snapping off of valve heads (or tips)—an event that can easily be triggered by crooked valve seating (guide wear, face/seat deposits). Not a pleasant prospect, especially for turbocharged engines, where a broken exhaust valve can mean a turbo overhaul. (Valve shrapnel, on its way out the engine, usually goes though the turbo rotor.)

Damping action can be destroyed in several ways. For example: a tappet plunger—if it becomes magnetized—can remain bottomed out in the tappet body permanently, giving rise to the foregoing scenario. (Plungers become magnetized through mechanics' removing tappets from engines with the aid of magnets—a procedure frowned on by the engine manufacturers.) Advanced wear can also cause a tappet to lose damping action—although this is generally a long-term process, preceded by a slightly faster-than-normal bleed-down rate (often detectable as engine roughness and/or a noisy engine). On a twin, too rapid lifter bleed-down can be noticed as a split in manifold pressures. (With turbocharging, the effect is less noticeable.) On a single, look for high manifold pressure at idle.

Another way to find yourself with collapsed lifters, or tappets that bleed down too rapidly, is to let a shop take your lifters apart during maintenance and put them back together in random order. (Believe it or not, it happens.) Hydraulic tappet components are not interchangeable; you can't assemble plunger No.1 into lifter body No. 4. Lifter

Continental-type hydraulic lifters are checked for the proper bleed-down rate by inserting the dry plunger assembly (minus the spring) into the barrel and then tapping the plunger with a screwdriver. If the plunger kicks back, the assembly is good. If it falls to the bottom of the barrel, the lifter is defective.

assemblies must be kept together, as a unit (and replaced as a unit— when a plunger is scored, you throw away the whole assembly).

Lifters are not a mandatory replacement item at major overhaul; they can be reused indefinitely, provided they bleed down at a normal rate. But when a camshaft is reground during a major, Lycoming and Continental require that new lifters be used. "New cam, new lifters" has been the rule for many years. But now, the FAA approves the use of reconditioned lifters in place of new ones.

REMOVAL, INSPECTION, AND REPLACEMENT

What do you do when you suspect that you are having lifter problems (as evidenced by roughness at high rpm accompanied, possibly, by loss of power and/or misfiring)? You pull the lifters in question, naturally, but not until you've eliminated all other possible contributors to the "rough engine" problem, such as faulty ignition harness components, bad spark plugs, plugged injector nozzles, and so forth. Ignition problems and lifter problems often mimic each other (defective spark plugs frequently will fire okay under low power conditions, but not fire—or fire poorly—under conditions of high cylinder pressure). There's no sense going to the trouble of pulling lifters if your problem is—or conceivably could be—with the spark plugs.

But if you do suspect a lifter problem, here's what you'll do: First, remove the valve cover from the cylinder(s) in question, then turn the crankshaft so as to find top dead center on the compression stroke (this relieves spring tension on the valves). Proceed to remove the rocker arms from their shafts, pull the pushrods from their tubes and take the pushrod housings out. On Continental engines, you'll need to push hard against the housing with a blunt tool in order to get it to clear the cylinder head. Be sure to catch the housing seals and washers as the shroud pulls free.

At this point, the intake and exhaust tappets will be visible through their respective holes in the crankcase. To remove them, fashion your own tappet-puller from a piece of .040-inch safety wire, hook the wire into the end of the lifter, and pull gently. Be very careful not to drop a lifter on the ground. Also, work on only one lifter at a time—you definitely don't want to get any lifters mixed up. (Lycoming sells a special tool, P/N 64941, designed to make lifter-pulling easy.) Avoid using strong magnets to pull lifters out. Repeated use of a magnet in this fashion can cause the tappet plunger to become magnetized, leading to defective tappet operation. (This may, in fact, be the source of your problem: Check for previous magnetizing of the tappet by holding a dimestore-type compass next to it. If the tappet is magnetized, reject it.)

Before going any further, take a look at the tappet face (the surface that rides against the cam). Use a magnifying lens, if possible. The main things to check for are spalling, pitting, radial scores, and goove wear, any of which are cause for rejection of the entire tappet. (The finding of any of these conditions is also cause for close inspection of the lobes on your camshaft.) Groove wear indicates that the tappet has not been rotating in its hole, as it is designed to do. Spalling or pitting indicates a lubrication-breakdown problem (or, depending on what model engine you have, a long-standing design problem at the factory). Remember: If your eyes are good, you may find one or two *Rockwell marks* on each tappet face—this is the normal result of hardness testing at the factory. Do not confuse Rockwell marks with spalling or pitting.

If you see concentric rings of discoloration on the face of each tappet, again, don't worry—it's normal. (You're looking at varnish patterns created during the normal circular wearing-in of the cam against the tappet.) Only if you can feel waves or grooves as you run your fingertips over the metal have you got problems.

Now flip the tappet over and examine the concave end. Normal wear is indicated by a mirror polish at the bottom. (No generalizations can be made about the normal size or shape of the mirror area; it varies from tappet to tappet.) Any grooves or roughness that can be felt with your finger are cause for rejection of the entire tappet.

And when we say rejection of the entire tappet, we mean just that. With hydraulic tappets, there's no such thing as throwing away a *part* of one, or salvaging parts from two tappets in order to make one good one. *The bleed-down rate of the tappets is critical.* Mixing plungers and bodies will wreak havoc with bleed rates and clearances, so don't even give it a thought. When in doubt, reject the assembly.

Speaking of bleed-down rates, if you're wondering just how the bleed rate is checked, it's simple: First, disassemble the lifter completely (again, working on only one unit at a time, to avoid mixing parts). Next, thoroughly clean all parts in unused solvent—preferably naphtha or acetone. (Stoddard solvent and kerosene are definitely not recommended, since they leave a rather thick film residue.) Note: If carbon has formed in the tappet body, making it difficult for you to remove the plunger, this may be the source of your problem. Excess gum or carbon here means you've been using an inferior oil and/or waiting too long between oil changes.

Lycoming tappets are checked for bleed rate by holding the hydraulic cylinder between thumb and middle finger—placing the plunger in position so that it just enters the cylinder—and depressing the plunger quickly with the index finger, observing whether the plunger immediately kicks back. Lack of "kick" means the leakdown rate is excessive and the lifter must be rejected. (This test is to be conducted with all parts *dry*.) Note: Lycoming requires that when a lifter is found to be defective, the associated valve must also be replaced (see paragraph 6-55d, page 6-13. Avco Lycoming direct-drive *Overhaul Manual*).

Continental lifters are designed somewhat differently from Lycoming lifters, but the bleed-rate test is performed in a similar manner. Start with the tappet barrel sitting open-end-up on a flat surface. (Again, make sure all parts are *clean and dry*.) See that the large expanding spring is removed from the plunger. Start the dry plunger and valve assembly into the bore. It should fall to the level of the barrel oil hole and stop. Now give a good inward tap to the plunger assembly with a screwdriver. The plunger should kick back promptly due to the compression of trapped air beneath it. By successive taps, you will be able to work the plunger all the way in (this is normal)—but the initial kickback should indicate good compression. If not, you've got a defective lifter.

If your tappets pass the foregoing test, and there are no indications of cracks, gouges, obvious wear steps, or other damage to any tappet components, your tappets are reusable. Reassemble the parts (oil them lightly) in the reverse sequence of steps followed during disassembly. (Do not fill the tappets with oil, however; they will receive proper lubrication in the engine.) Likewise, after inserting the lifters in the crankcase holes from which they came, reinstall all remaining valve-train components, verify that everything appears to be working correctly (normal valve action with prop rotation) and replace the rocker covers, using new gaskets.

Tip: If you don't have access to a pushrod-housing spring compressor during reassembly, *safety-wire* those stout shroud springs in the compressed position, then *cut* the safety wire when you're ready to "snap" the shrouds into final position.

One more thing: Don't reinstall those pushrods without *filling them with oil first*. Installing pushrods dry can cause rockers and valves to starve for oil during the first seconds of engine startup, as engine oil slowly makes its way through the empty rods.

For more information on the subect of hydraulic tappets, consult your engine overhaul manual and talk to your mechanic. (Remember, you'll need his signature in your engine logbook, if you intend to do any of this work yourself.) We can only give you *part* of what you need to know here. The rest you'll have to learn by doing!

THE REGROUND LIFTER CONTROVERSY

In late 1985, a major controversy developed over the "remanufacturing" or "field-reconditioning" of hydraulic valve lifters. In view of the potential harm to engines involved as well as the larger principles of parts standards, the issue is well worth reviewing.

The FAA had granted approval to numerous shops to regrind camshafts, and some of those facilities also gained FAA approval to

The badly spalled lifter on the left—compared to the normal lifter face on the right—indicates the type of damage that can occur when improper grinding is done. Both lifters are from the same Lycoming O-320-H2AD. The flyspeck marks on the good lifter are from a Rockwell test.

remachine lifters. If lifters are ground incorrectly, an owner can end up with an engine full of metal chips (to say nothing of a ruined camshaft) in no time. And, according to Avco Lycoming, that's what many customers were getting. In March and May of 1985, Lycoming issued two service letters (L206 and L206A) advising operators *to avoid field-reconditioned lifters at all costs.*

Protection Versus Economies

Offhand, you might not think there would be much of a market for something as esotric as remanufactured lifters, but in a general aviation fleet of 191,000 American piston aircraft—as of 1985—of which 25,000 are twin-engined, you have well over *two million* lifters on active duty. If only ten percent come in for overhaul each year, that's still a fair number of lifters—enough to support a strong rebuilt-lifter market.

The financial incentive to use reground lifters is substantial. Whereas a single lifter can cost upwards of $60 new (with a six-cylinder engine containing 12 lifters, that's almost $1,000 per engine), the same item can be bought for $10, reconditioned and yellow-tagged.

But has Lycoming been right? Are reground lifters to be avoided, no matter what? Has the FAA unwittingly put its seal of approval on a risky procedure? Or is Lycoming taking an unduly protectionist position? With more and more mechanics and engine shops sending tappets out with camshafts to be reground (in an effort to reduce overhaul costs—and increase profit margins), the answers assume tremendous financial, if not safety, significance.

Neither Lycoming nor Continental regrinds lifters at the factory in the course of rebuilding engines for the "zero time factory reman" market—and neither manufacturer will pick up the tab when a customer's engine chews up a camshaft after installation of field-reconditioned lifters. But because many of the reground tappets that gave trouble bore Lycoming pat numbers, Lycoming inevitably found itself on the receiving end of a number of complaints. Lycoming decided to deal with the situation by issuing Service Letter L206, strongly condemning the use of reconditioned tappets. The letter said, in part: "Our investigation shows that using remanufactured tappet bodies/cam followers often leads to camshaft and tappet body prob-

This mushroom-style Lycoming 72877 lifter shows considerable spalling at the face. To remove this style of lifter from an engine requires crankcase separation.

lems in a very short time, thereby necessitating their removal and replacement. Severe wear or spalling of the cam lobes and tappets can result in metal particles contaminating the oil supply. Avco Lycoming continues to recommend that any time a camshaft and/or tappets are replaced, only new Avco Lycoming tappets be installed."

More than one person we talked to in the tappet-reconditioning business scoffed at the Lycoming service letter, saying, "Well, of course they'd like you to buy new Lycoming lifters—just like they also want you to buy all your valves and rings from Lycoming, and not from Superior."

But there's a big difference between an aftermarket (PMA) exhaust valve that's made by the same vendor, to the same specs, as the OEM valve, and an OEM lifter body that has had metal taken off it and offered as "remanufactured." As one expert in the lifter-reconditioning business told us, "You don't just start grinding away at the face of one of these things—there are some fairly critical material properties and dimensional characteristics that have to be maintained, and if you don't know what you're doing you can get into trouble real fast."

Critical Properties

Exactly what are the mysterious dimensional and material properties that must be maintained in a lifter? "For one thing," ECI (Engine Components, Inc.) president Gary Garvens told *Light Plane Maintenance*, "there is a curvature on the face of the lifter body, where it meets the cam lobe. This curvature is very small—it's invisible to the naked eye—but it's absolutely vital that it be there because of the fact that the cam lobe itself is tapered or ground on a slant. When we regrind a lifter, we restore the proper radius to the lifter face, and check it with an optical comparitor to *make sure* the radius is the same as for a new part. This is a very important step in the reconditioning of lifters, and I can tell you that not all of the remanufactured lifters out there on the market today are offered with this radius intact. That's part of the problem."

A spokesman for AEA (Aircraft Engine and Acessory Co.) in Dallas confirmed this. "Keeping the proper curvature on the face of the tappet body is an important part of what we do, and you need special equipment to do it. We actually maintain an elliptical contour, with the aid of special grinding equipment, similar to lens grinding equipment."

A typical cam lobe taper might be five thousandths of an inch of slant per inch of lobe width, and a corresponding lifter face radius might be 30 inches. These dimensions change with normal wear during the course of an engine's TBO life (and that's one reason the manufacturers warn not to mix old and new lifters and camshafts haphazardly).

ECI claims to maintain new tolerances (not only for face curvature but for overall O.D., body length, etc.) on all of its remanufactured lifters—a feat that might seem impossible, considering that a "used" lifter doesn't grow in service, and can only shrink when metal is removed in the regrinding process. But as ECI's materials chief Gary Greenwood told us, "There's a lot of beef on these parts to begin with, and after you shave a few ten-thousandths off you find you're still well within new tolerances—no problem." Besides which, hydraulic lifters are self-adjusting; a few thousandths of an inch of shank length makes no difference to the operation of the lifter. "It's really academic anyway," Greenwood points out, "when you consider that you select pushrods by length when you build up an engine. And those pushrods can vary a heck of a lot more than a few thousandths of an inch."

Because the cam lobe rubs against a rounded lifter face, the force of overcoming valve spring pressure (and combustion pressure) is concentrated in a tiny patch on the lifter surface. The peak pressure at the cam-lobe/lifter interface can be as high as 100,000 psi. Surface finish and hardness at the lifter face are thus critical.

Metal has been smeared off the lobes of this camshaft. The center lobe in this photo operates both intake lifters for the forward cylinders of an O-320. Note the off-center wear.

According to Lycoming, some lifter regrinding firms are not maintaining the proper surface finish or hardness on reground lifter bodies. FAA's New York certification office reviewed Lycoming's complaints and failed to find merit in them; FAA hasn't acted to revoke its approval from any firm involved in lifter rework.

AEA, ECI, and Precision Air Parts all take steps to restore the proper surface finish (6 micro-inches) and Rockwell hardness to reconditioned lifters after grinding. For purposes of ensuring proper wear-in, ECI and Precision subject lifters to Parko-Lubrite processing, while AEA applies Ferroxing. All three firms check lifters for Rockwell harness at several points before regrinding as well as after. (Lifters are also 100-percent magnetic particle inspected before being released for service.)

Our Recommendation

Just as most engine overhaulers will use aftermarket parts from Superior or Engine Components in the rebuilding of a customer's engine unless the customer specifies Lycoming or Continental factory parts, there is a growing trend of overhaul agencies to use reconditioned lifters rather than new ones (sending the lifters out to be reground with the cam)—unless the customer specifies otherwise. This is one area where it pays to be an educated—and picky—customer. It's one thing to put an engine together with brand-new (not reconditioned) aftermarket valves or pistons. When it comes to reconditioned (remachined) parts, especially precision-machined parts such as hydraulic lifters, extra caution is in order.

Hydraulic lifters are *not* a mandatory-replacement item at overhaul (either for Lycoming or Continental engines). If camshaft regrinding is done, however, we would recommend *against* simply reinstalling old lifters. Ideally, the firm that regrinds the cam ought, also, to be the firm that regrinds the lifter. Do we recommend lifter regrinding? Let's put it this way: When down by a properly equipped shop with an FAA approved lifter-reworking regimen, we believe lifter reconditioning is a reliable and cost-effective alternative to buying new parts from the original-equipment manufacturer (OEM).

The bottom line: If your engine is down for major—or soon will be—be sure your mechanic knows a Parko-Lubrited, properly radiused (not to mention Magnafluxed and yellow-tagged) hydraulic lifter from a hole in the ground. Lycoming just may be right on this one; there's more to a lifter than meets the eye.

Part III
IGNITION

Chapter 6

SPARK PLUG INSPECTION

If we were forced to choose the one area of preventive maintenance that offers the aircraft owner the greatest financial return on the smallest investment of time, money and effort, our pick would have to be spark plug maintenance.

By involving yourself closely in monitoring and maintaining the condition of your plugs, you can save on unnecessary shop labor, prolong the life of your plugs and even be able to gauge the general health of the engine with surprising accuracy in detecting minor induction, liner-wear and other problems before they assume major proportions. Just knowing that you *don't* have to replace plugs with those your mechanic offers at inflated, retail prices but can safely go the discount route can save you some 40 percent on plug maintenance.

If you've asumed that spark plug maintenance is too unimportant (and/or boring, and/or inexpensive) to justify your participation, this chapter could stimulate some beneficial changes.

PRELIMINARY MAINTENANCE QUESTIONS

Spark plugs can be unduly costly not only in acquisition costs but in downtime associated with periodic cleaning, regapping, and rotation. One reason for this is that aircraft spark plugs are unique. They're absurdly big, they're heavy, and they're expensive. In fact, they are so different from the familiar, puny plugs in our automobiles that many an otherwise mechanically capable owner/operator shies away from handling aircraft plugs, abandoning the field to the A&Ps, who certainly don't assume this "burden" for nothing.

Working on your plane's plugs is both safe and legal, as long as you avoid the classic no-nos, which we will point out as we go along. The first taboo is working with the wrong tools, out of misplaced frugality or financial overexuberance.

The Right Stuff

There's no sense in even attempting to become involved in spark plug maintenance unless you have the right tools. By "right" we mean:

[1] a high-quality torque wrench;

[2] a six-point 7/8-inch deep socket that will fit aviation plugs;

[3] a 3/4-inch or 7/8-inch open-end wrench for loosening ignition-lead terminal nuts;

[4] a plug tray;

[5] wire-type feeler gages;

[6] a thread clean-out tool (for steel and brass bushings only);

[7] unleaded gasoline with which to clean spark plug threads and ignition terminal sleeves;

[8] a supply of Bon Ami (for cleaning the inside of plug shielding barrels);

[9] a handful of new 18mm copper spark plug gaskets;

[10] thread anti-seize compound.

If you don't already own a good torque wrench, get one now. Any good dial-type or deflecting beam torque wrench will do fine, but if

Removing and servicing your own spark plugs is legal and cost effective, if proper care and the appropriate tools are used.

you can afford it we strongly recommend that you buy a micro-adjustable, ratcheting, 3/8-inch square drive torque wrench such as the one offered by AC Spark Plug under Model Number ST-110. Dial and beam-type wrenches have the limitation of being difficult to read and use properly in tight spaces (the bottom plug on the number six cylinder of a Bonanza, for instance). The torque-limiting feature and flexing head of the ST-110 eliminate such problems.

Along with the torque wrench, you'll need a deep socket. Champion offers a magnetic socket made especially for aviation plugs. We consider this a waste of money. Check with local hardware and auto parts stores to see if you can't locate an ordinary six-point 7/8-inch deep socket that will accommodate an aircraft plug. (Hint: Take an old plug with you when you go looking for a socket; many so-called "deep" sockets aren't deep enough for aviaiton plugs.) If you encounter difficulty locating a 7/8 deep socket with 3/8-inch drive, opt for 1/2-inch drive and a 3/8-inch to 1/2-inch adapter.

The only advantage of buying the Champion CT-430 deep socket is that it's magnetic, and it *may* keep you from dropping a plug on the floor someday. (A dropped plug is automatically a nonusable one.) In our experience, a non-magnetic socket, carefully used, is just as good (and a lot less expensive).

Do you absolutely *have* to have a plug tray? If you want to be able to cart a lot of plugs around safely, without dropping (and thus ruining) them—and if you want to be able to judge engine health at a glance by comparing top and bottom spark plugs from all cylinders, all at once—then our answer is "yes." We recommend Champion's CT-446 tray.

Champion and AC both offer wire-type feeler gages for aviation plugs (Champion's CT-450 is the better buy), but any two-buck automotive-type set of feelers will do, so long as they're of the straight-wire variety and so long as they cover the .016- to .022-inch range of gaps used for aircraft plugs. (Many automotive gages *do not* adequately cover this range.)

If you know for sure that your engine's spark plug bushings are made of brass or steel, you should plan on buying a thread clean-out tool eventually, to use to keep debris from falling out of your spark plug holes and into the cylinders during routine plug maintenance. Champion and AC both offer thread clean-out tools.

If you know for sure that your cylinders have helicoil inserts instead of machined spark plug bushings—or if you're not sure what kind of bushings you have—*do not* buy a thread clean-out tool. (Such a tool can cause damage to and/or backing out of the helicoil inserts in your cylinders, leading to expensive repairs.) A stiff-bristled toothbrush, coated with bearing grease, will do a fair job of cleaning out helicoil inserts.

The question of whether or not to buy and use anti-seize compound for aircraft spark plugs is a old one. The plug manufacturers say that

Among the tools that facilitate safe spark plug removal are (left to right) a spark plug socket with a knuckle and extension, a 7/8-inch combination wrench, a ratchet handle and a torque wrench.

you should use the stuff; many mechanics, on the other hand, prefer to use engine oil (or the residual grease left by the thread-cleaning tool) to lubricate spark plug threads prior to reinstallation. Frankly, at only a few bucks a bottle (enough to last a couple years), we don't see why anyone would *not* want to use an anti-seize compound. Use engine oil at your own risk. (Oil won't always keep a hot-running plug from freezing in its bushing.)

Spark Plugs: Where and When to Buy Them

The time to buy new spark plugs is not when your old ones wear out, but while your old ones have some life left. By buying a new set of plugs now and keeping them handy, you'll be able to replace your old plugs with the new ones when plug-cleaning time rolls around, allowing you to keep your plane in service while you rejuvenate the old plugs at your leisure. Also, by buying new plugs now you'll be able to beat future price increases.

Whatever you do, *don't* let a mechanic do your plug shopping for you. A&Ps love nothing more than to screw a few new plugs into an engine at annual-inspection time, and screw the plane-owner by charging him full list price for the plugs (which he probably didn't need anyway; mechanics often retire plugs prematurely). Don't let this happen. There's no reason for you to have to pay full list retail for *any* spark plug.

How can you beat high prices? One way is to switch to Bendix Autolite plugs, which are just as good as Champions or ACs as far as the FAA is concerned, but cost somewhat less. (Massive-electrode Autolites list at about 20 percent less than their Champion counterparts.) Another sure way to beat the high prices is to buy from a dealer who discounts spark plugs. If you can find a dealer who discounts *Autolite* plugs, you've got it made.

How can you know what kind of plugs to order? One thing you definitely do *not* want to do is simply examine the plugs you're now using and order identical replacements. Plugs come in several different heat ranges and barrel designs, and it is quite possible that whoever installed your last set of plugs installed the *wrong kind* of plugs. Don't simply repeat the last man's mistakes.

To determine which kind of plug is specifically recommended for your engine, consult the appropriate manufacturer's Spark Plug Application service bulletin (Teledyne Continental S.B. M77-10 or Lycoming S.I. 1042). Alternatively, go to the service department of any large FBO and ask to see a Champion, AC, or Bendix Autolite plug application chart. You'll find that while many different models of spark plugs will *work* in your engine, only one model will be *specifically recommended* for your engine—usually a massive-electrode (not an exotic) type. This is the kind of plug you should order.

How Often to Service Your Plugs

Many aircraft service manuals (including the Mooney M20C through J, Piper PA28/28R, and Cessna 150/172/182 manuals) advise operators to service spark plugs every 100 hours *or* at each annual inspection, whichever comes first. As far as we're concerned, this is nonsense.

Unless your engine is brand new and you're operating on platinum or iridium plugs—or you have some other reason for believing that your plugs don't need more frequent servicing—you should pull your plugs at least once every 50 hours, even more often, if fouling is a persistent problem. Once every 100 hours may be fine for those of us who run air taxi operations and are logging 50 hours a month; in the real world, however, aviation plugs (especially *bottom*-hole plugs) need more frequent attention than that, especially if the engine in question is old, and/or 100LL fuel is being used in place of 80-octane, and/or the engine in your plane is not being flown much (i.e., less than 15 hours per month).

Let's not lose sight of why spark plugs need to be pulled periodically in the first place. There are three basic reasons:

[1] Electrode gaps tend to grow with time, due to the extremely corrosive conditions prevalent in the combustion chamber and the constant arcing between the electrodes. As the electrodes erode—and the gap between them grows—ever-higher voltages must be produced by the magneto to induce sparking, and the chance of connector-well flashover increases. (Hard starting also becomes a problem as gaps grow.) The rate of electrode wear varies greatly from plane to plane, so it is impossible to predict just how often *you* will have to regap *your* plugs. But the point is, your plugs *will* have to be gapped periodically, and it is important that you check gap growth often.

[2] Lead and carbon buildup can be very rapid for some engine types; operated improperly, *any* engine can accumulate enormous amounts of lead and/or carbon on its plugs. (On engines with severe ring, cylinder-wall, or valve-guide wear, oil fouling can also be a problem.) To avoid the possibility of misfiring, preignition, etc. (and

A Champion spark plug cleaning bench. Note the highly useful wire-type feeler gage.

the attendant engine damage), it is important that such electrode deposits be removed periodically. In addition, it is important—for long plug life—to *catch lead buildup in its early stages,* since advanced lead fouling is often ineradicable and can necessitate early plug retirement.

[3] To achieve long spark plug life, it is essential that plugs be periodically *rotated top to bottom (and bottom to top) in firing sequence,* to counteract the tendency of bottom plugs to become oil-fouled *and to prevent abnormal electrode wear caused by long-term constant-polarity discharge.* In case you didn't know it, every ignition lead coming from a given magneto fires with an electrical polarity opposite that of the lead firing before (or after) it. For any given ignition lead, the polarity doesn't change—and, over a period of time, this can cause abnormal electrode wear.

If a plug repeatedly fires with *positive* polarity, the ground electrodes will wear faster than the center electrode; conversely, if the plug always fires *negatively,* the center electrode tends to wear out first. To achieve balanced electrode wear, it's necessary to "rotate" spark plugs between top and bottom holes, and between even and odd numbered cylinders, at regular intervals.

There are other reasons, of course, for removing the plugs from your engine periodically—such as to inspect the plugs for serious damage, signs of flashover, etc.—but we consider the above considerations to be primary in importance. If any of your plugs begin to crack apart or short out, you'll know about it in short order. But the only way you're going to find out whether your plugs' electrodes are wearing abnormally, or whether carbon fouling is beginning to be a problem in the left bank of cylinders (indicating an induction problem), or whether lead oxide deposits are threatening to send your plugs to an early grave, is to *pull and inspect (and rotate) your plugs religiously every 50 hours*—more often, if conditions warrant.

How Old Is Too Old?

Throw away your spark plugs when any of their electrodes have worn to 50 percent of their original thickness. On an Auburn plug, the center electrode will look like a Mazda engine rotor; on a massive Champion, the center electrode will assume the shape of a football. (Don't just look at the center electrode, however. Also check the ground electrodes.)

It goes without saying that you should also throw away plugs when damage of any kind is evident. Cracked center ceramic can be especially dangerous. In radial-engine days, before modern ceramic recipes were perfected, fragments of ceramic would sometimes break free and (trapped by the ground electrodes) rattle around in the firing end of a plug. The chip of ceramic would become extremely hot and set off preignition, often resulting in an engine fire. A number of airliners suffered this problem.

How much life you get out of a plug will depend on many factors, including combustion chamber design, leaning technique, air filter maintenance, the type of fuel used, whether or not TCP additive is used, etc. Under reasonable best-case conditions, a set of massive Auburns or Champions can be expected to last 600 hours or more. Some fine-wire types have gone as much as 2,000 hours. (Don't expect to be able to do that in a 152 or Tomahawk, however. Lead fouling is not "cured" by switching to fine-wire plugs.)

Plugs and Bum Raps

Spark plugs, as anyone involved in the sale or manufacture of igniters will tell you, are often wrongly blamed for a variety of ills. Complain to a busy A&P of a rough runup, for example, and the first thing he'll probably do is remove all your spark plugs. If one or more plugs are wet and black, chances are good you'll be offered the

Owners of Cessna 172s and other prominent singles have been assured through service manuals that spark plugs need servicing no more frequently than every 100 flight hours or each annual inspection—not a realistic suggestion for such aircraft, if they are, typically, relatively infrequently flown.

opportunity to buy new ones. Chances are also good that your runup problem will still exist.

If you read the standard picture-matchup spark-plug diagnosis leaflets, they all say that if a plug is wet and black, it's oil-fouled (which it is). But the mere fact that a plug is oil-grimy doesn't tell you how it got that way. Is it not firing because it's oily? Or is it oily because it's not firing? It could be either.

Consider what has to happen in order for a spark plug to fire. For ignition to occur, a voltage has to be generated across the plug electrodes of sufficient magnitude that arcing will occur. Anyone who has shuffled across a carpeted room, only to be zapped by a door knob, knows this principle. (The gaps involved are about the same, too.) The greater the distance the spark is required to jump, the greater the voltage that will be required for arcing. By the same token, if you insulate the gap—with air, oil, carbon, or what have you—a greater voltage will be required for arcing. Pressures inside a cylinder prior to ignition are often several times atmospheric; hence, several times more total voltage is required to spark the gap in a cylinder than on an open-air test bench. (Hence the significance of the so-called bomb-test apparatus, which pressurizes plugs prior to electrical testing.)

High-tension magnetos are capable of developing 12,000 volts or more in the secondary winding, which is sufficient to cause a fairly large gap to arc in normal conditions, but achieving that voltage at the spark plug electrodes is frequently another matter. Resistance build-ups can and do occur at either end of an ignition wire; and voltage leakages can occur in between. When you remove the terminal leads from your spark plugs, examine the spring contact. If it looks crusty or burnt, you're looking at an unnecessarily high resistance that has to be overcome by your magneto before the spark plug will spark. Likewise, eroded gaps and deposit buildups in firing cavities also rob arcing power from spark plugs (hence the need for periodic cleaning and gapping).

A brand-new spark plug gapped to .016-inch in an airplane with a new, clean, non-leaky ignition harness might need, say, only 2,000 volts to fire in normal cruise operation. In service, as the gap opens up, the same plug will need greater voltage to fire. With normal (minimal) carbon and lead buildup, that plug will require even more voltage to fire. Let some corrosion develop in the terminal well—or let a defect develop in the ignition wire itself—and the voltage requirement might shoot up to 5,000 volts or more. At high altitude, where ambient

The gray/white ash-like appearance of this platinum plug indicates a lean-operating cylinder. Despite the fact that the electrodes show a little wear, this $25 plug was discarded by a mechanic.

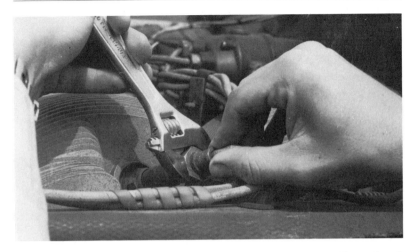

When you loosen the terminal hex, hold the ignition elbow with one hand, to keep it from turning.

air pressure is low (but cylinder pressures are still high, especially in a turbocharged engine), the voltage required to spark the plug might exceed the voltage necessary for internal shorting to occur in the magneto, giving rise to high-altitude misfire.

The insidious thing about the above scenario is that when a well-intentioned mechanic installs new spark plugs in your engine, it will run fine again at high altitude (for a while), tending to confirm the mechanic's suspicion that "it was the plugs."

It *isn't* always the plugs. Remember that a partially clogged injector nozzle—by interfering with combustion—can cause a cylinder to pump oil and make the spark plugs wet, in a fuel-injected engine. Similarly, advanced ring wear makes for oily spark plugs (and attendant misfiring under high-demand conditions)—as does reduced compression for *any* reason (valve leakage, etc.).

PLUG INSPECTION AND ENGINE HEALTH

In the face of so many ills and so strong a possibility of misdiagnosis, the only sensible recourse is to pull the plugs and inspect them.

Removing the Plugs

Removing spark plugs from an aircraft engine is neither difficult nor unsafe (even for a rank amateur) as long as certain rules are followed. We've already discussed the need to use the correct tools.

You will want to start, of course, by removing as much of the cowling as you need to in order to get at both top and bottom plugs. (This is a whole chapter by itself, for some planes.) Next, walk up to a plug and—using either a 3/4- or 7/8-inch open-end wrench (depending on what kind of ignition lead you have)—begin to loosen the terminal nut at the top of the plug.

If you find that a 7/8-inch wrench does the job here, it means you have "all-weather" ignition leads and plugs—so called because the plugs' shielding barrels have been designed in such a way as to accept a resilient grommet which forms a water-tight seal to keep moisture out of the barrel area. All-weather plugs have 3/4-inch diameter shielding threads with a pitch of 20 turns per inch. If you find that your terminal nuts have a 3/4-inch hex, it means your spark plugs' shielding threads are of the 5/8-inch 24 variety and your ignition leads are of the older, non-all-weather type. (Have non-all-weather leads converted over to all-weather leads at your next engine overhaul.)

Once you've got the terminal hex "started," hold the ignition lead steady in one hand (to prevent its twisting) while you loosen the terminal nut with your other hand. Then *pull the lead assembly straight out of the shielding barrel,* being careful not to exert side pressure against the insulation lug, or "cigaret." (Also, do not touch the spring or cigaret with you fingers; the salts on your skin are highly conductive and could—if left on the terminal sleeve assembly—cause a short circuit to ground.)

Note: If you encounter difficulty getting the cigaret to pull out, twist it slightly (as if you were going to unscrew it) as you pull. The seal should break easily.

To remove the spark plug, place your deep socket on the plug (being sure it completely covers the plug hex), attach a long-handled ratchet, steady the socket with one hand so that it doesn't cock over and damage the plug, and (with your other hand) exert a steady pressure on the wrench handle. Don't use a torque wrench for this step; the extreme forces that are often necessary to unscrew a plug will throw the wrench's calibration off.

Once the plug has begun to rotate freely, remove the wrench handle and unscrew the socket by hand. As you reach the last couple of threads, carefully withdraw the socket and grab the plug in your hand, being certain not to let the plug fall to the ground. *If you drop a plug, throw it away*. A dropped plug—if it is not already cracked inside—may fail in flight later; it cannot be reused.

Preliminary Examination

When all of the plugs you intend to work on have been removed in the above manner, give them a good preliminary examination for damage and/or wear. Inspect shell and barrel threads for damage; shell hex for rounded corners or other mutilation: center electrode ceramic for chips or cracks; firing end of plug for severe damage (e.g., copper runout); and all electrodes for severe wear. Any of the foregoing conditions is cause for retirement of the plug in question (with the exception of minor thread damage, which can be repaired by an A&P).

If any electrodes are missing, or if copper runout is evident at the center electrode, you should assume that preignition and/or detonation has occurred in the cylinder from which the damaged plug came. Quite possibly, you're looking a top overhaul in the face. Have a mechanic examine the jug with his borescope.

Damaged leads, such as the one shown above, can badly hinder engine performance. Terminal cavities and ignition leads should be inspected whenever plugs are removed.

How worn must the electrodes be before you have to toss a well-used (but otherwise sound) plug into the garbage? The plug manufacturers say that any time the ground *or* the center electrodes wear to half their original thickness, the plug should be retired. (This goes for exotic-metal as well as massive-electrode plugs.) Generally, when a massive center electrode goes out of round by .030-inch or more, you can be sure the plug is shot.

Any time a spark plug is removed from an engine—and particularly a malfunctioning engine—it should be closely inspected (in its original, "as removed" state) to see what clues, if any, the plug might give as to the engine's (or individual cylinder's) state of health. Spark plugs do indeed tell a story—if you know what to look for.

After the initial inspection for damage and wear, arrange the plugs in a plug tray by cylinder and by cylinder position (top and bottom).

First, keep in mind that a certain amount of oil on an engine's *bottom* plugs is considered normal. Oil on your cylinders' *top* plugs, however, spells trouble. Generally, it is a telltale sign of ring or cylinder-wall wear. (If you're considering buying a plane that's at or near its TBO, pull all the top plugs after your first demo ride; they'll tell you the whole story.) Oil on the top plugs means that an engine overhaul is not far off—particularly if oil consumption is high and cylinder compression is less than encouraging.

Terminal Cavity and Ignition Leads

Spark plug terminal ends (and ignition lead connectors) should come in for close scrutiny whenever plugs are removed from an engine. Misfiring is just as detrimental at this end of the plug as it is at the other end. Many operators seem to have forgotten this.

Start with the ignition lead terminal. In "all weather" or 3/4-20 type terminals, the insulator sleeve has an exposed edge or end, which should carefully (so as not to leave fingerprints) be inspected for evidence of carbon tracks. These will appear as heavy lead pencil lines across the entire width of the end of the insulator sleeve and indicate that the ignition lead connector, which was attached to the spark plug, may be defective. This permits electrical discharge to the metal part of the spark plug shield.

Misfiring of the spark plug, induced by the defective connector, will be noticed during take-off and climb engine operations, or at high altitudes, and may not be encountered during ground operation or with new spark plugs.

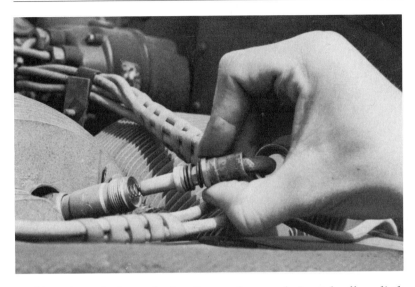

Problems in a plug's terminal well may show up during takeoff or climb (or at high altitude) but may go totally unnoticed during ground runups. Such problems often disappear after the terminal lead is cleaned with MEK and the contact spring is dressed up with very fine sandpaper.

Short leads preventing a positive contact between the contact spring and the contact gap in the spark plug may cause the engine to misfire during take-off and climb operation and, in extreme cases, during low power, especially with lean mixtures.

Cross-firing in the magneto distributor can also produce spark plug insulator failure and piston distress.

The bottom of the insulator well around the contact cap location should be inspected for the presence of black contamination on the walls and also at the contact cap. Black soot-like deposits usually indicate that the insulation of the ignition lead has been exposed to temperatures above normal.

Damage From Excessive Temperatures

Overheating of the spark plug barrel, sometimes caused by damaged cylinder baffles or missing cooling air blast tubes, may seriously deteriorate the ignition leads. Any overheating of the spark plug barrel by a defective baffle or exhaust gas leakage at the exhaust pipe mounting flange can generate temperatures in the insulator tip sufficient to cause preignition and piston distress.

Interpreting Color of Insulator Tip Deposits

The firing end of the spark plug should be inspected for color of the deposits, cracked insulator tips and gap size. The electrodes should be inspected for signs of foreign object damage and the massive type also for copper run-out.

The normal color of the deposits usually is brownish-grey or gray tinted slightly with red. These colors are most prevalent, but there may be a different color combination which would be normal for the type of operation the spark plugs have been exposed to.

Dull and smooth black deposits on the insulator tip usually indicate that the spark plug is lead carbon fouled. This type of spark plug fouling is caused by incomplete combustion; it usually results from improper ground operation when the engine is cold, and is more prevalent when the atmosphere is cold and very humid. It can also happen in a cylinder with weak compression, an engine with a defective primer solenoid, or in a cylinder that is using excessive amounts of oil. In many instances, if both spark plugs are affected, the deposits will not burn off under normal engine burn-out procedure, making replacement of spark plugs necessary.

Black, with some glaze or irregular formation and of sufficient amounts to short out the spark plugs, usually indicates prolonged ground operation with a very rich carburetor setting, followed by a sudden increase in power output. This causes a rapid increase of the insulator tip temperature and prevents the deposit formation from being vaporized. This type of spark plug fouling is more prevalent in float equipped aircraft.

Orange-yellow and glaze appearing deposits on the insulator tip usually indicate that the spark plugs have been exposed to higher than normal temperatures as happens when detonation is experienced.

An ash-grey colored surface or chalk-white surface on the insulator tip and the exposed metal parts, indicates that the spark plug was exposed to very high combustion chamber temperatures, usually caused by severe detonation or preignition. The free end of the side electrodes on fine wire spark plugs will be of a bluish-gray color and free of any accumulation of deposits. In massive type spark plugs, evidence of copper run-out could be visible.

The cylinders from which spark plugs with the above conditions were found should be inspected with the aid of a borescope. It may be desirable to replace the cylinder, especially if backfiring has occurred.

Watching for and knowing the meaning of various colored deposits can reveal a great deal about how your engine is working.

The reason for this precautionary action is that if the engine was operated under some detonation conditions, but not to the extent that it caused a complete piston failure, the piston rings could be broken and a piston failure requiring a complete engine change may show up at a later date.

A black-colored deposit on the spark plug gasket and the gasket flange indicates that the spark plug was insufficiently torqued, allowing combustion chamber gases to leak past the spark plug threads. In aircraft engines using helicoil inserts, it may also cause a helicoil burnout.

Cylinders in which spark plugs with cracked insulator tips have been found should be thoroughly inspected for damage due to abnormal combustion chamber conditions, even though the ceramic separation could have been caused by improper installation procedures, improper methods used to check or reset the gap, or from being dropped. The electrode gap size should be inspected for uniformity and the electrodes for signs of distortion and nicks.

Besides cracked insulator and lead carbon fouling, spark plugs may also be made inoperative by ice or oil bridging of the electrodes; and if both spark plugs are affected in the same cylinder, it usually requires replacement. Spark plugs with fine wire electrodes are less susceptible to this form of malfunction due to the smaller surfaces available to collect the moisture or oil.

Electrode Gaps

The size of the electrode gap has a very definite effect on spark plug service life and also on the performance of the engine. Insufficient gap size will not only cause misfiring during idle, but will also misfire during cruise power with lean fuel/air mixture. This intermittent misfiring during cruise lowers the temperature of the insulator tip to such an extent that lead deposits forming on the insulators may not vaporize sufficiently to keep the tips clean.

All this information represents a service rendered by your plugs to tell you about the current welfare of your engine (and vice versa). To be fully cost-effective, you should proceed with returning the favor and servicing the plugs, which is described in chapter 7.

Chapter 7

SERVICING SPARK PLUGS

It should now be clear that, if you're interested in saving serious amounts of money on spark plug maintenance, it helps to know how to pull and rotate plugs yourself every 50 (or fewer) hours. It also helps to be aware that you can buy new plugs safely at discount and to know how to judge for yourself whether or not your old plugs are reusable—something your mechanic may not be in a position to judge objectively.

REMOVING FOUL MATTER

That is not where the story ends, however. We emphasize that there is much more to spark plug maintenance than merely playing "musical cylinders" every so many hours. Periodic *reconditioning* of your

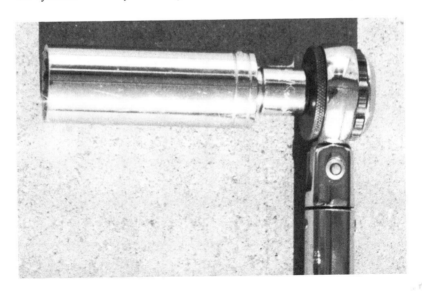

plugs is just as important as rotation/inspection. Reconditioning includes a wide range of cleaning, gapping and testing operations and is, for the plane owner oriented to servicing for himself what the law allows, an area rife with money-saving possibilities.

Cleaning Your Own Plugs

Reconditioning begins with a thorough cleaning of each plug. (Only *after* a plug has been subjected to cleaning operations can the electrodes—which are partially worn away by blast-cleaning—be gapped, and the plug itself bomb-tested.) Generally, this means degreasing the firing end of each plug, blast-cleaning the electrodes, manually removing any deposits deep in the firing end cavity that cannot be removed by abrasive blasting, cleaning (with a wire brush) all plug threads, and (if need be) cleaning out the inside of the shielding barrel.

If this (admittedly long) list of cleaning operations intimidates you—just relax. In the first place, you won't always need to go through these cleaning operations (or for that matter, *any* reconditioning procedures) at every 50-hour plug rotation; these operations are to be carried out only when (and as) conditions warrant. (Chances are, your

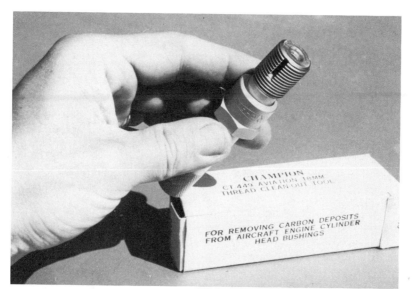

Do not use a thread chaser to clean helicoil inserts; a toothbrush is better.

plugs won't need cleaning—or reconditioning—more than once or twice a year.) And in the second place, there's nothing at all difficult about cleaning a spark plug. Any of the following operations can be carried out easily and quickly, in the privacy of your own garage.

First things first: If the firing ends of your plugs look greasy or oily, wash the oily parts off with Varsol, Stoddard solvent, unleaded gasoline, or dry-cleaner's naphtha. (The accepted procedure here is to place the plugs in a tray, firing ends down, and set the tray in a container filled two inches deep with solvent, then wait 30 minutes.) Whatever you do, *don't* submerge the plugs completely in the solvent; you don't want the fluid to enter the shielding barrel. And *don't* use any solvent other than the four listed. (These four solvents are the only ones specifically recommended for plug degreasing by AC and Champion.) Note: After the plugs have been degreased, blow dry them with compressed air or dry them in a 200°F oven.

When the electrodes are dry, they're ready for abrasive blast-cleaning. Here, you have three options: [1] Hire a mechanic to do this job for you; [2] find a shop that's willing to let you use their plug cleaning machine; [3] invest in your own plug-cleaning equipment.

Don't give up on option no. 2 too quickly; it's not as hard as you might think to find a shop that'll let you use their plug blaster and related equipment, particularly if you check the one- and two-man shops (at remote airports) first. Many mechanics who would sooner cut off your hands than lend you a screwdriver are not at all unhappy to let a perfect stranger use their abrasive blast machine (since they know you won't be able to walk off with it).

Caution: Blasting

If you have access to compressed air and a torque wrench, you can reap the advantages of do-it-yourself plug cleaning. For less than $20, you can buy a Vixen portable abrasive blast-cleaner.

Perhaps you've seen your mechanic wield one of these handheld sandblasters before. If not, you'll be amazed at how simple the device is to use—and what a bangup job it does of ridding the barnacles from a spark plug's firing cavity. All you need to do is couple the unit to any source of compressed air (100 psi from an air tank will do), insert a spark plug into the neoprene grommet in the end of the cleaner, ensure that the Vixen's canvas bag is filled with an adequate (3/4-pound or so) supply of Crisilite abrasive (which comes with the unit), flip the air valve lever to the "B" (for Blast) position, and press the go button just behind the canvas bag. For best results, rock or swivel the plug from side to side. After five to ten seconds, flip the air valve lever from "B" to "A" (air), and—once more—hit the button. (This step blows all the loose abrasive powder out of the firing cavity of the plug, thus keeping Crisilite out of your engine.) That's all there is to it.

Of course, if your spark plugs are visibly wet with oil, you'll probably want to take a moment, before you begin, to soak the electrodes in unleaded gasoline (or Varsol, or whatever petroleum distillate you have on hand), then dry them with compressed air. Otherwise, when you go to blast-clean the (oil-fouled) plug, you'll tend to dirty up the machine's abrasive powder rather quickly, clumping the individual granules and reducing cleaning efficiency to zip.

All in all, the Vixen portable blast-cleaner does an excellent job of turning crusty electrodes into clean ones (so does a turbocharger, incidentally), but it is important to remember—with devices of this sort—that there *can* definitely be too much of a good thing. Sandblasting unavoidably removes a certain amount of electrode metal (and therefore service life) from plugs. Ten to 15 seconds of abrasive blasting per cleaning session, per plug, should thus be considered about the limit, if you want to get several hundred hours out of your plugs. It is often said—no doubt correctly—that more aircraft spark plugs are worn out on abrasive blast machines than in engines.

If the lead buildup is moderate to severe, abrasive blasting alone isn't going to do the trick. After you've blasted the electrodes clean, you're going to need to go after deposits deep inside the firing end cavity. Usually, this is done with the aid of a vibrating tool of one sort or another (AC and Champion have their respective versions), but— according to one mechanic—the job can be done just as well (though not as quickly) using a homemade tool. "Just get yourself a hacksaw blade," the A&P told us, "and grind it on the non-serrated side so that the blade tapers to a long, sharp point. Then you can poke the blade inside the end of the plug and use it to break up deposits on the ceramic insulator."

Of course, if you take care to operate your engine in such a way as to eliminate lead fouling (see discussion later in this chapter) and inspect your spark plugs often enough to detect lead buildup in its early stages, you should never need to go to the above lengths to clean your plugs—abrasive blasting will be all you'll ever need.

Once the firing ends of your plugs have been blasted and (if necessary) vibrator-cleaned, give them a thorough blow-out with

"Instant-cleaning" your spark plugs on the ramp with a wild and woolly runup may impress people for miles around, but it isn't likely to bring you good results.

compressed air. Then check the condition of the 18-mm shelf threads and—if need be—clean them with a wire brush to remove caked-on carbon, grit, anti-seize compound, etc. If you use a power-driven brush for this step, be careful not to let the brush touch the electrodes.

At this point, it is generally considered good practice to clean the terminal well of each plug (although many mechanics are inclined to omit this step if the terminal well looks sanitary). To do this, insert a cotton swab moistened with methanol, Stoddard solvent, or methyl-ethylketone into the barrel of each plug and rotate the swab a couple of times. (If solvent alone will not remove persistent stains, you can use Bon Ami or Aloxite as an abrasive cleanser. Do not, however, use other products—and in no case should you use carbon tetrachloride as the cleaning solvent.) Blow out the plugs with compressed air when your're finished.

Cleaning by Burnoff—Good or Bad?

It can happen that, for one reason or another, a rough runup may signal you to clean your spark plugs right then and there. Many pilots like to try to "burn the plugs clean" on the taxiway—a holdover from radial-engine days. The technique is usually for the pilot to decide that he's "got some plug fouling" and then to wind the tach up to 2,000 rpm while he inches back on the mixture control. The entire airplane seems to vibrate, straining at its locked brakes. Perhaps grass clippings fly by. Perhaps passengers' fillings rattle loose.

High-rpm plug burnoffs are bad for propellers (abrasion damage), bad for nose-gear oleos (debris damage from prop blast), stir up dust (some of which unavoidably gets into the engine, since no filter is 100-percent efficient), and overheat engine compartments. But the main problem with the technique is that, quite often, it doesn't work.

Many things can cause a rough mag drop—including bad harness wires, poor terminal spring contact at either end of the lead, or glitches involving the magneto itself. It can even be an airframe vibration anomaly. (In one case, a CFI aborted a flight because of a bad runup in a Tomahawk. On making the taxi-turn to go back to the ramp, the left gear leg fell off.) Running the engine to tooth-rattling rpms on the ground while fiddling with the mixture control won't do a thing to make a bad ignition lead good again. (Or put a gear leg back on.)

Foul Penalties

But suppose it *is* genuine electrode fouling. (Not that you could ever know for sure, even with the best EGT system.) How can you know what *kind* of fouling it is? There are at least three different kinds of fouling to contend with, and not all can be "burned off."

Lead fouling is the most familiar type of plug contamination. It's also the most persistent. Lead oxide (which forms BB-like globules inside the plug firing cavity) melts at 1,630° Fahrenheit. (Its boiling point is much higher.) You aren't going to "burn off" lead deposits on the taxiway. Generally, if lead buildup has progressed to the point where it is affecting your runups, it's too late to attempt "burning the deposits away" on the ground; you might as well try wishing them away. The only remedy at this point is to remove the plugs and floss them.

Carbon fouling—which gives a spark plug a dry, sooty-black firing end—is prevalent in aircraft that spend a lot of time idling or operating super-rich, at low power settings (i.e., trainer aircraft). Carbon deposits "evaporate" at temperatures above 900° Fahrenheit, though, so you might be able to burn off some carbon by running up to 2,000 rpm for a few seconds. Trouble is, it might take a lot more than just a few seconds to remove the carbon from your plugs this way. And running up at 2,000 rpm on the ground for more than a few seconds is not a good idea. (If carbon fouling is a persistent problem, adjust your idle mixture.

Oil fouling is what most pilots have "burned off" when they succeed in burning off "plug deposits." This kind of fouling gives rise to visible wetness (oil) on the electrodes of plugs—wetness that causes electrodes to short out. Plugs can become oleaginous in either of two ways: 1. excessive oil in the combustion chamber (from severe ring or barrel wear). 2. normal runoff from cylinder walls between flights. In either case, bottom-hole plugs will be more affected than top-hole plugs, simply due to the effect of gravity.

If your engine is passing fairly large quantities of oil (a quart every two hours, say), or if one or more jugs are pumping oil for some reason (that is, the top-hole plugs are wet along with the bottom plugs), you can expect rough mag drops on a frequent basis. It's going to be a fact of life until you do a top overhaul.

Leaning and Frequent Flying

You can also expect plug fouling during runup if you're in the habit of going a week or more between flights. (This is particularly true for planes with canted engines, such as Barons and 310s.) Runoff oil accumulates in the low point of the cylinder barrel and sloshes onto bottom plugs on the first startup after a long inactive period. While you're taxiing to the runup area, the engine runs smoothly because the top plugs are dry. It's only when you select single-mag operation that things go to pot. (In case you didn't know, each mag fires half of your top plugs and half of your bottom plugs.)

If your problem is oily electrodes, a brief burnoff just may do the trick. Open the throttle to about 2,000 rpm, lean the mixture slowly until an rpm drop is noted, then enrichen to the point of smoothness. Hold it there for 10 seconds. Then enrichen and repeat the mag check. *If the roughness persists, taxi back in and investigate the cause.* Don't sit there on the taxiway repeating the leanout until you (and your valves) are blue in the face.

In fact, don't even try the burnoff technique unless you're on intimate terms with the aircraft and are 90-percent certain the problem is plug oiling. If you've got any other kind of plug (or engine) distress, you'll only be wasting your time, and TBO, performing high-rpm leanouts.

A far better technique is prevention. That means *leaning during taxi*; leaning in flight whenever the engine is below 75-percent power; frequent flying; and regular plug cleanings. (Start with 25-hour intervals and go up or down from there.) TCP fuel additive will also do wonders for extending TBRR (time between rough runups) if you're burning leaded fuel (of any octane), but by far the most important single thing you can do is lean the engine properly.

ELIMINATING LEAD FOULING

Most experts argue that the single largest causative factor in early spark plug retirement is lead oxide accumulation. When plugs accumulate lead, they have to be serviced (i.e., blast-cleaned) more often—and when plugs are serviced often, they wear out more rapidly. (In 250 hours of operation, a plug may be subjected to as many as 10 or 12 blast-cleanings, enough to utterly demolish *any* set of electrodes.) Of course, if lead-fouled plugs *aren't* serviced often, lead buildup can proceed so rapidly that the plugs may—in less than 100 hours—become fouled beyond all hope of reconditioning. Next thing you know, you're shelling out for new plugs again. And again. And again.

It doesn't have to be that way. Here, as always, a gram of prevention is worth a kilo of cure.

Operational Techniques

There are several operational "tricks" that you can employ to reduce lead fouling in your engine. Ten of the better-known (and more effective) techniques for the elimination of lead buildup are to be found in Avco Lycoming Service Letter No. L192, dated March 15, 1979. Here are their recommendations:

1. By use of the spark plug recommendation charts, be certain the proper plugs are installed. Do not simply replace the same part number of those removed. A previous mechanic may have installed the wrong plugs.

2. Do not accept an overrich carburetor or fuel injector at idle or off idle engine speeds. Have a mechanic adjust the mixture.

3. After a flooded start, slowly run the engine to high power to burn off harmful lead deposits, then return the engine to normal power.

4. When parked for any reason, avoid closed throttle idle. Set engine at 1,200 rpm. The fuel contains a lead scavenging agent, but it only functions with a spark plug nose core temperature of 800° F or higher. To have a minimum of 800° nose core temperature you must have a minimum of 1,200 engine rpm. Also, the engine will run cooler and smoother, and the alternator/generator will have more output at 1,200 rpm. (Taxiing is exempt. Accept whatever rpm is required.)

5. Use the normal recommended leaning technique at cruise condi-

Infrequently flown airplanes with canted engines, including the Cessna 310 and Beech Baron, are susceptible to plug fouling during runups.

tions regardless of altitude and re-lean the mixture with application of alternate air or carburetor heat. If the aircraft is used as a trainer, schedule cross-country operations whenever possible.

6. Avoid fast, low-power let downs from altitude whenever possible. Plan ahead. Descend with power. (Avoid overrich conditions.)

7. Avoid closed throttle landing approaches whenever possible. Use a slight amount of power. Remember carburetors and fuel injectors are set slightly rich at closed throttle.

8. Keep engine operating temperatures in the normal operating range. Too many people think the lower the temperatures the better. Keep cylinder head temperatures in normal operating range by use of normal power and proper leaning and use oil cooler baffles to keep oil temperature up in winter.

9. Swap top and bottom spark plugs every 25 to 50 hours. Top plugs scavenge better than bottom.

10. After flight or ground operations and before shut down, go to 1,800 rpm for 15 to 20 seconds, reduce to 1,200 rpm, then shut engine off immediately with mixture control.

The Mechanics of Lead Fouling

The techniques just listed need no particular elaboration here, except to say that we feel very strongly about points 2, 5, 9 and 10, which have received too little emphasis in published discussions of lead fouling. It would probably serve the reader's interests better for us to discuss briefly the *mechanics* of lead fouling and to suggest some tactics not mentioned in the Lycoming service letter and not generally known to aircraft owners and pilots.

Many pilots have come to believe that lead buildup on spark plugs is an unavoidable fact of piston-engine life—that the rate of lead accumulation is, in fact, directly related to the amount of lead in the fuel. This is not strictly correct. Ethylene dibromide—a very potent lead scavenger—is added to all aviation gasolines in the precise chemical proportions necessary to fully scavenge (or carry away) the amount of lead present. Given a chance to do its job, ethylene dibromide can very effectively prevent lead buildup on spark plugs (and elsewhere in the combustion chamber). For various reasons, however, ethylene dibromide is not always allowed to do its job.

One reason that ethylene dibromide does not always scavenge efficiently is that—in order for it to work at all—spark plug tip temperatures of 800° F or more must be maintained, and during low-rpm operation this is not possible.

A far more significant problem, as it turns out, is maldistribution of tetra-ethyl lead (TEL) and ethylene dibromide in the induction system. Ethylene dibromide has a boiling point of 265°F; the boiling point of TEL is about 390°F. (Gasoline, of course, is a heterogeneous mixture of substances and has no single "boiling temperature." *Most* of the hydrocarbons in gasoline, though, have a boiling point close to that of ethylene dibromide.) Because of this dissimilarity in boiling temperatures, some degree of fractionalization of fuel components can (and does) occur in your plane's induction system. Thus, less-volatile fuel heavy ends rich in TEL may—under certain circumstances—go almost entirely to one or two cylinders, while ethylene dibromide (by virtue of its greater volatility) may be distributed more evenly. The result is that, in some cylinders, a huge excess of TEL (relative to ethyene dibromide) can develop, leading to massive lead fouling of the plugs in those cylinders.

Obviously, one way to deal with the problem of TEL maldistribution is to raise the temperature of the induction air, thereby aiding vaporization of the fuel components. On carburetor-equipped engines, this can be accomplished quite effectively with judicious use of carb heat. Turbocharging also helps (as does the proper use of cowl flaps).

In case you've ever wondered why lead fouling occurs more rapidly in cold weather, now you know. Fuel fractionalization is the key.

Still another (very significant) factor in the development of lead fouling is the introduction of *liquid* gasoline into the cylinder that can occur occasionally not only with carbureted engines but with fuel-injected ones as well. With a carbureted powerplant, it is sometimes possible—under conditions of reduced induction airflow—for tiny droplets of liquid fuel to form in the manifold. (Because TEL is slow to vaporize, these droplets can be very high in lead content and very low in scavenger content.) Once ingested into the cylinder, said droplets tend to fall to the lowest point in the combustion chamber—the bottom spark plug—and form beads of lead oxide there during combustion.

Fuel injected engines are not immune to this phenomenon. The problem is that—in the typical continuous-flow system—the fuel-air charge is being drawn into the cylinder throughout only about one third of the cylinder's operating cycle. The other two thirds of the time, the spray of fuel goes into the intake port with the intake valve closed. Hence, it is sometimes possible (particularly under conditions of low-cylinder-temp operation) for liquid fuel (again, high in TEL) to accumulate in the intake manifold and result in bottom plug fouling.

This is why *bottom* plugs frequently accumulate more lead than *top* plugs.

Maintaining Adequate Scavenging

You'll notice that most of the techniques outlined in Lycoming's Service Letter L192 are aimed at creating (within the cylinder) the conditions most favorable to efficient lead scavenging by ethylene dibromide. They do not address the seemingly more intractable problem of *how to eliminate lead fouling when there is a high ratio of TEL to scavenger in one or more cylinders* (which, as we have seen, is an important factor in lead buildup). Obviously, if there's not enough scavenger present to do the job, it doesn't matter how you lean the engine—you're still going to have leftover lead. The question is, what can you do to correct this situation?

The answer: Add more scavenger to your fuel. The reason the

refineries don't already do this for you (the reason Exxon doesn't put two or three times as much ethylene dibromide in its avgas as it already does) is that bromide is chemically very "active" (i.e., corrosive). In other words, an excess of bromine would be more harmful to your engine than an excess of lead.

But ethylene dibromide is not the only lead scavenging agent around; tricresyl phosphate (TCP) also scavenges lead effectively, and has the advantage over ethylene dibromide of not being corrosive. Which brings us to our final recommendation on the reduction of lead fouling (and, we think, one of the most important, cost-effective recommendations we can give any plane-owner who wants to save money on maintenance): If you're not now using TCP in your fuel—and you've been experiencing lead fouling—*start using it*—regardless of whether or not your engine was originally designed for 100-octane gas. (Note: This recommendation does *not* extend to turbocharged engines.) *Any* normally aspirated engine that experiences lead fouling of its spark plugs will benefit (in many ways) from the addition of TCP to its fuel, no matter what the octane rating of the fuel. This has been shown by a variety of studies.

TCP concentrate is available from many FBOs (or directly from Alcor. (One gallon will suffice to treat about 1,240 gallons of 100LL avgas.)

Needless to say, lead fouling is a complex phenomenon, much more so than it first appears. (Certainly, it defies adequate description in the space available here.) For now, it's simply enough to know that there *are* effective techniques available for reducing lead buildup on spark plugs (the most reliable of which is to add extra scavenger—in the form of TCP—to your fuel), and that by applying these techniques diligently you can double or triple spark plug life.

GAPPING

Different operators inevitably experience different rates of electrode wear, so it is impossible to predict how often you will have to gap your plugs. (Some would say that a pilot's—or a mechanic's—abrasive blast-cleaning technique has more to do with how often plugs need to be regapped than anything else.) In any case, you will probably find that your plugs do not need to be regapped very often—which is just as well, given the expense of the equipment necessary to gap aviation spark plugs.

Gapping-Cost Gaps

Due to their unusual two- and three-prong electrode designs, aviation plugs are not as easily gapped as automotive plugs. Special equipment is necessary, and the plug manufacturers have seen to it that this equipment is not cheap.

There are three ways to get around the high cost of gapping equipment. One is to have your plugs gapped by a technician, at

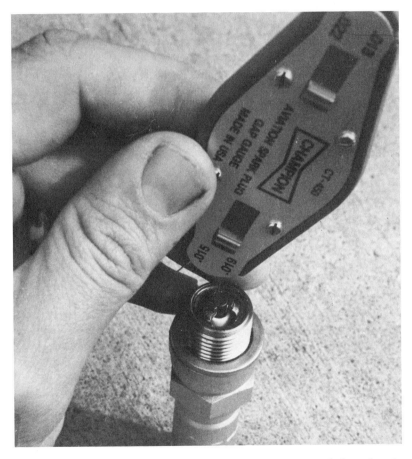

When checking electrode gaps, it is customary to use two feeler wires to judge the "nominal gap" of the electrodes. For a nominal gap of .016-inch, the .015- and .019-inch wires of the Champion CT-450 gap gage are used. For a nominal gap of .019-inch, the .018- and .022-inch probes will be used.

nominal cost. Another possibility is to do the work yourself using someone else's equipment. A third way is to buy your own equipment—but not through aviation suppliers. If you do a little checking, you'll find that many of the same gadgets that are regularly sold to pilots and mechanics at unconscionably high prices are available (from the same manufacturers, but under different stock numbers) on the automotive aftermarket at *substantially reduced prices*. For instance, Champion's CT-415 massive-electrode plug gapping tool exists in automotive circles as the CT-415B and in that form sells for two-thirds the price of the aviation model.

A tool that can do what more expensive AC and Champion tools will do and that costs little more than $10 is the Sure-Gap spark plug gapper, marketed by the Aircraft Tool Supply Company, of Oscoda, Michigan.

It is small enough (less than two inches from handle to handle) to fit in one's pocket and is simple in design: a half-inch-long segment of one-inch O.D. steel, bored out and threaded to accept a standard 18 mm aviation spark plug. Four evenly spaced holes have been drilled around the circumference of the body: two T-handle "adjusters" are provided in opposite holes. These adjusters are what close the electrode gaps of the spark plug when the tool is in use.

From the way the thumb-screws are arranged around the circumference of the tool, you might suspect that the Sure-Gap has been designed only for use with two- and four-prong spark plugs. Actually, it is not. Three-prong AC and Autolite plugs are accommodated by the Sure-Gap; you simply adjust one electrode at a time, in the case of three-prong plugs.

Using the Sure-Gap is a cinch. First, screw the tool down onto the business end of the saprk plug you're interested in gapping. The idea is to turn the tool down to where the T-handle adjusters are aligned— radially, and vertically—with both electrodes of a standard two-electrode (Champion) plug. (If the adjusters are too high, or too low, they can be brought into position by rotating the entire tool a half or quarter-turn right or left.) Once the adjusters are properly aligned, you can begin turning each T handle clockwise to move the ground electrodes closer to the center electrode. (This is best done very slowly, one adjuster at a time. A quarter turn of the T handle suffices to close the electrode gap .006-inch.) Every few seconds, you can loosen the T handles and check the electrode gap with a wire-type feeler. When you've reached the gap stated in your aircraft service manual (generally somewhere between .016- and .022-inch, depending on magneto output and engine compression), you can unscrew the Sure-Gap from the plug and go on to the next plug.

There is another way to get around the high cost of gapping tools, and that is to switch over to fine-wire (exotic metal) plugs. It turns out that the equipment needed to set the gap of platinum or iridium electrodes is much less elaborate (and expensive) than the corresponding equipment for massive electrodes. (AC's AV2-1 tool acts as both gapper and feeler gage for fine-wire plugs, and is inexpensive.) We don't recommend that you go this route, however, partly because we're not fans of exotic-metal plugs and partly because platinum and iridium (being very brittle substances) tend to break rather than bend. (Don't be surprised if the electrodes fall off in your hand the first time you try to adjust the gap of a fine-wire plug.)

Precautions in Gapping

The essential things to remember about setting electrode gaps are:

1. Always adjust electrode clearances with your feeler gage *removed* from the gap, so you won't inadvertently apply a side loading to the center electrode.

2. Move the outer electrodes only. Again, you should *never* apply a side load to the center electrode.

3. Plug gaps should be adjusted *after* (not before) cleaning operations, since cleaning tends to open the gap somewhat.

4. Never open a gap that has been closed too much. Bending the outer (ground) electrodes back and forth is forbidden. According to Champion, gaps that have been closed up to .004-inch beyond specs can be kept in service; but if you blow it by more than .004-inch, the plug should be scrapped (or reworked by a competent technician).

5. Adjust electrode clearance to the *lower* side of the permitted range of gaps. That way, you'll be able to fly more hours between regappings (among other benefits). (Gaps always open up—they never close—in service.) There are important disadvantages to the use of low gap settings (.015- to .018-inch), however. The narrowness of the gap is limited by the demand for a strong spark created by adverse engine-starting conditions. In other words, if you set your gaps much below .019-inch, you may (under certain conditions) experience some difficulty starting your engine. Also, you will increase the risk (or speed the onset) of lean misfire, during lean-cruise operation. As a result,

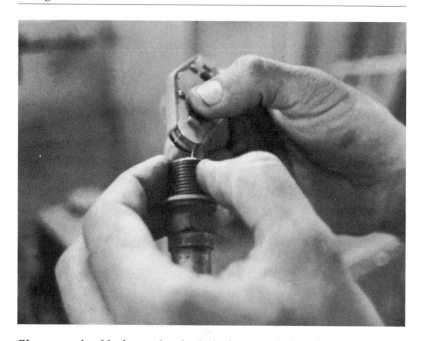

Plug gaps should always be checked after, *not before, blast-cleaning.*

you'll have to fly with a richer cruise mixture setting than you otherwise have used.

Lycoming states that plug gaps "shall be set to .016-.021-inch." Continental, in its plug bulletin (M77-10), allows .015-.018-inch gaps *or* a gap of .019-.022-inch, stating that "the larger gap is generally preferred for improved starting and idling characteristics." Then why use the smaller gaps? Chiefly for more consistent operation at high altitudes.

If you fly a turbo-something, you'll want to set somewhat smaller gaps than your normally aspirated friends use. Smaller gaps are easier to fire and put less stress on magnetos.

If you don't know what the accepted range of gaps is for your plugs, consult your aircraft service manual or call the factory. (Spark plug application charts will give you an accepted "nominal value" for each type of plug, but will not furnish a *range* of recommended gaps for your engine and ignition system, as your aircraft manual will.) If you're installing brand new plugs—and you've ordered the right type for your engine—the new plugs will come already gapped, with the gap stated on the package label. You shouldn't have to gap a new plug.

Electrical Testing of Plugs

"Electrical testing," says one text on aircraft ignition, "consists of assuring yourself that the spark plug will spark in the gap under pressure." One might presume from the wording of this statement that if you are already safisfied that a given spark plug *will* perform its job properly, electrical testing of the plug need not be conducted. This is, in fact, the attitude that many (if not most) mechanics have on the subject. It is our atitude as well, since the FAA nowhere states (in any of its publications) that electrical testing *must* be conducted as part of routine spark plug maintenance.

Unless your plugs have been subjected to rough handling—or you have some other reason to suspect that they may not perform normally when put back into service—you can forget about putting your plugs on the test stand each and every time you have them out for servicing. Rather than test your plugs at every 25- or 50-hour rotation, it makes more sense to bomb-test them once at every *reconditioning* interval (i.e., once every 100, 150, or 200 hours). This is something either you or your mechanic can do, using a shop's equipment or your own.

The procedure is simple and involves little more than screwing a spark plug finger-tight into the tester, pressing a button and opening an air valve while observing the plug through a small window. If it sparks continuously under pressure, the plug is deemed "good"; if it sparks intermittently or not at all, it goes into the garbage pail.

Many pilots are confused about the proper interpretation of bomb-test results. Should all electrodes fire evenly? How weak is "weak firing"? When should a plug be rejected?

Forget about all the electrodes firing evenly—you'll rarely, if ever, see that, and it's not important in any case. The outer electrodes are *paths to ground*. Whichever outer electrode provides the easiest path ("the path of least resistance," if you like) will provide sparking action. *Sparking causes ionization and wearing away of metal*, so eventually the gap will open up on the electrode pair that is (initially) doing all the work. This will in turn increase its resistance and cause another electrode pair to be favored. *That* pair will fire repeatedly until *its* gap opens, causing the other electrode(s) to fire again, etc. In other words, the spark will alternate (in an irregular way) between electrode pairs. This is normal.

Still, at least one electrode pair *should arc consistently* when juice is applied to the tester, under pressure. If the discharge is at only one electrode pair *and* is irregular or "weak" (ask your A&P to show you what that looks like), either rework the plug until it fires normally (i.e., deep-clean the firing cavity some more), or reject the plug.

REINSTALLATION AND FINAL STEPS

The reinstallation of spark plugs in an aircraft engine calls for a good deal of common sense—mistakes can be costly—so watch what you're doing—*and proceed slowly.*

Consider the Holes

First of all, remember that you're not going to want to put the plugs back in the same holes they came from (or into just any hole, randomly). As mentioned earlier, it's necessary—if you want to minimize the effects of asymmetric (constant-polarity) electrode wear—to rotate plugs from top to bottom *and to the next cylinder in the firing order* when reinstalling them. It's usually possible to do this simply by rotating the plugs in sequence on the ignition leads of a given magneto; study your plane's ignition harness(es) to confirm this. (Have you kept track of which plug came from which hole in which cylinder? This is where a plug tray becomes indispensible.)

Before installing any plugs, check the cleanliness of the individual cylinder openings; any holes that are obviously unsanitary ought to be cleaned out. Steel or brass bushings are best cleaned with a thread chaser. (Apply grease to the notches in the side of the tool before you begin; this will keep debris from falling into the combustion chamber.) If your cylinders employ helicoil inserts (look for a small tang at the top of the threaded opening), *do not use a thread chaser.* Instead, clean up the inserts as best you can with a lightly greased toothbrush.

Gaskets

The next thing to do—assuming you're dealing with reconditioned plugs, rather than new ones—is put new copper gaskets on the plugs. (Brand new plugs, of course, already come with new gaskets.) Old gaskets should not be reused, since [1] they are likely to be misshapen and [2] they will have become hard or brittle through use. The chances of a reused gasket forming an imperfect seal are small, but the consequences of a bad seal (plug seizure, thread damage, preignition) are sufficiently grave as to outweigh any financial benefit to be gained by reusing old gaskets. New gaskets cost about less than a quarter apiece. Use them.

Copper gaskets harden in service. They also assume a conical shape, due to the fact that the spark plug bottom flange has a two-degree angle built in. If you reinstall old, hardened gaskets convex-side-up, you may not get a good seal. The cone shape (which will flatten and "go the other way" when the plug is installed) will contribute to drag torque, perhaps allowing you to reach 30 foot-pounds prematurely—especially if the threads are unlubed and still caked with dirt (or worse, dented from handling damage).

Lycoming, in its plug bulletin (S.I. 1042Q), says to "always use new gaskets" (P/N STD-295). Accepted industry practice, however, is to reuse gaskets *if the gaskets are properly annealed*. If you plan on reusing gaskets, anneal them by heating them to cherry-red with a propane (or other) torch. This stress-relieves the copper and returns the gasket to a soft condition which will allow proper sealing of the plug, which of course is the gasket's intended purpose.

Thread Lube

Now is the time to apply anti-seize compound (or a little engine oil) to the threads of each plug. (Again, we're assuming you're working with reconditioned plugs. *New* plugs come prelubricated.) Remember to apply the compound sparingly and to start the application a full thread away from the firing end. If you get any of the copound on any of the electrodes, you might as well throw the plug away; the stuff causes permanent fouling. (You can't burn it off.)

New plugs come prelubed with lightweight oil. Many mechanics like to dab a little engine oil on reused plugs just prior to installation. Others use Champion P/N 2612 thread lube on plugs (in accordance with Champion's own recommendations). A sizable—and loud—sub-group of mechanics likes to pooh-pooh Champion's graphited thread lube, however, pointing (with some justification) to the fact that an excess of graphite on the end of a spark plug can quickly lead to misfiring, if electrodes are bridged.

We side with Champion on this one. The graphited thread lube is preferable to engine oil, because it doesn't break down at high temperature to form gluelike varnish or carbon (as oil does). Graphite, incidentally, isn't the only active ingredient in graphited thread lube"; a small amount of mica is also used to provide thermostabile lubrication. Remember, you don't just want the plug to go in easily—you also want it to *come out* easily at the next service period.

Do follow Champion's warning, however, and *be absolutely sure* that no excess of lube can run off onto electrodes after plug installation. This means starting the lube application a full thread away from the firing end. And don't apply too much of the stuff. We like to apply one brush-load (one drop, essentially) of Champion 2612 to each plug, in three or four equally spaced "wipes" along the thread walls.

Remember to shake the bottle before wetting your brush. Mica and graphite do not remain in suspension very long.

Torque

At this point you're ready to install your plugs. Start by screwing each plug all the way into its bushing by hand. (If it won't turn all the way down by hand, something's wrong. Either the bushing threads are still dirty or some threads are damaged or you've managed to cross-thread the plug. Remove the plug and try again.) Be absolutely certain that there is one—and only one—gasket on each plug. If one of your cylinders uses a thermocouple gasket, omit the spark plug gasket for that hole.

Note: *Use extreme care* when screwing plugs into cylinder bushings, to avoid cross-threading the plugs. Cross-threading will result in expensive cylinder repairs.

Torquing each plug down is now a simple matter of placing your 7/8-inch deep socket over the plug (bottoming it on the shell hex), attaching a torque handle, and—as smoothly as possible—tightening the plug to the desired torque. If you own a Lycoming engine, the proper torque range is 30 to 35 foot-pounds; for Teledyne Continental products, the factory-recommended torque is 25 to 30 foot-pounds. (That's for all 18-mm aircraft plugs, regardless of reach, heat range, or type of electrodes. If you own an older aircraft that has 14-mm plugs, tighten them to between 20 and 25 foot-pounds—regardless of engine make.)

Plug torque is specified at 35 foot-pounds by Lycoming, 25 to 30 foot-pounds by Continental. Why the manufacturers differ on this, nobody quite knows. (The threads, after all, are the same in either case.) To our way of thinking, 30 foot-pounds is plenty. Plugs have a way of "tightening" in service (actually, they don't *tighten*—they just get harder to remove, due to carbon formation on threads), and if you overdo it on installation, you're just asking for trouble later on.

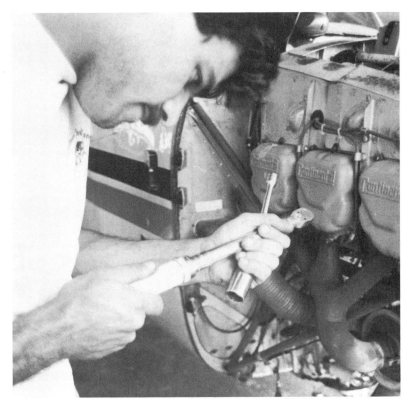

The soundness of your reinstallation will depend on your correctly setting the torque and also on your hand-screwing the plug down as far as it will go, using only plugs with undamaged threads and being careful not to overtighten.

But note one thing carefully. The above torque values are predicated on *lubed threads*—clean, undamaged, lubed threads. If threads—on the spark plug *or* in the cylinder head—are nicked, dirty or gritty, and/or completely dry, the plug will be installed with a drag torque that will "fool" you into reaching final torque prematurely. This, in turn, can be a source of real trouble later on. If a spark plug comes loose, you'll have a jet of exhaust gases burning threads, torching nearby ignition wiring, maybe even scorching cooling fins. Put a vented injector nozzle nearby, and you've got a recipe for disaster.

Don't fixate on torque-wrench indications. Rather, ensure that your wrench indications are *meaningful*—by cleaning and lubing threads properly, by ensuring that plugs go down all the way by hand before attaching the torque handle, by rejecting plugs with damaged threads, and by calibrating your torque handle frequently. (Ask your A&P when and where he gets *his* wrench calibrated.)

Checking Spring Contacts and the Cigaret

Before inserting the ignition lead in the plug, take a moment to wipe the cigaret (insulation plug) off with a clean cloth moistened in methanol, MEK, acetone, or unleaded gasoline. Also, check to be sure the cigaret is free of damage and that the inside of the plug shielding barrel is clean and dry. Then—without allowing your skin to touch the cigaret itself—carefully insert the connector assembly in the plug, in a straight line. Finally, screw the connector nut into place finger-tight (holding onto the ignition "elbow" so it doesn't turn) and use a wrench to tighten it an additional 1/8 of a turn. (Do not overtighten.)

It's amazing—and appalling—to see how many people (A&Ps and pilots alike) are willing to let corroded and burnt spring contacts pass inspection when installing plugs. You might want to check this on your next preflight; it only takes a minute. Just undo the ignition terminal hex at each plug (using a Crescent wrench, for example), pop the cigaret out, and eyeball the spring end of the lead. Remember not to let the ignition wire twist or rotate while undoing the terminal nut (which, chances are, somebody put on too tight to begin with).

All of the magneto's output has to pass the tip of the cigaret spring to get to the center electrode of the spark plug. (The spring bears against the tiny slot-head screw at the base of the spark plug terminal well.) If the tip of the spring is black and crusty, you're looking at a source of high resistance. The magneto, generally speaking, can and will generate voltages huge enough to pass this barrier. But why make the mag work any harder than necessary? If there's a path of lesser resistance upstream somewhere (in the mag or out the harness), sooner or later the juice is going to stop right there, at the spring. Why tempt fate? Clean the spring and give yourself a margin of safety.

Hold the cigaret with a clean towel (don't deposit perspiration salts on it) while you take a jeweler's file, sandpaper, emory paper, or even a Swiss army knife blade, to the crusty spring. (Make sure the spring is long enough to make good contact in the plug. If it looks short, extend it, or take the matter up with your A&P.) When the tip of the spring is shiny again, insert it back into the plug—and tighten the terminal hex *finger-tight plus one full flat* (60 degrees).

Final Testing

Spark plug maintenance does not end with the reinstallation of the properly serviced plugs. The only way you can know whether your servicing operations were successful (and did not accidentally result in damage to one or more plugs)—the only sure way to tell whether the reconditioned plugs are truly airworthy—is to run the engine up and perform an ignition system check.

As you perform you mag check, note the amount of rpm drop on either mag (there should be less of a drop than before, and the difference between mags should be less than 50 rpm); also, observe the sound and "feel" of the engine on either magneto. Rough single-mag operation tells you that one plug is "cutting out." If you have a multi-probe EGT, you'll be able to tell immediately which jug has the bad plug—and by virtue of the fact that you know which mag gave rough single-mag operation), you'll be able to tell which of the two plugs in that jug is defective.

If you don't have a multi-probe EGT—and you suspect you have a defective plug somewhere (but you don't know where)—you can pinpoint the errant igniter by simply running the engine a minute or two on the "rough" mag, shutting the engine down, and performing a "cold cylinder" test. (The older generation of mechanics would do this by spitting on each exhaust pipe. The pipe that doesn't hiss, of course, is connected to the cold cylinder.) Thus, if continuous operation on the right mag were to produce a cold number-four cylinder—and if you knew that the *right* magneto in your plane fires the *bottom* plugs in the *even*-numbered cylinders—you would know that the *bottom* plug in your number-four cylinder is bad.

We don't recommend that you actually perform the foregoing test to pinpoint the location of a misfiring plug, since [1] it is not good practice to continue to run an engine whose cylinders are not all firing, and [2] prolonged single-mag operation can (and will) produce severe fouling in the non-operating spark plugs. A far better approach is to monitor EGT indications.

The Log Entry

When you have satisfied yourself that your plugs (and ignition system) are in good working order, shut your engine down; then get out your engine log-book and make a detailed log entry stating the date, the tach time, the type of work accomplished, the fact that a runup check was successfully performed, and who did the work (e.g., "all work accomplished by owner/operator in accordance with FAR Part 43"). This entry will serve to remind you of when and why your last spark plug maintenance was accomplished (information that is all too easily forgotten if not recorded), and will also absolve others (i.e., hapless mechanics) of any responsibility for the quality of your work. If you have no qualms about the quality of your work, then you should have no qualms about making such a log entry.

Ignition Care for Rarefied Air

Many pilots—owners of Piper Turbo Arrow, Seneca II, and Mooney 231 aircraft, in particular—have discovered the hard way that ignition system defects are much more likely to manifest themselves at high altitudes than at low ones (a natural result of the tendency of electrical discharge—wanted or unwanted—to occur more readily in a vacuum than in a standard atmosphere). Increasing reports of engine roughness at and above 12,000 feet in the foregoing types of aircraft prompted Bendix's Electrical Components Division to issue a Service Bulletin (No. 612) establishing rigorous 500-hour cleaning and inspection guidelines for Bendix ignition system components.

Teledyne Continental addresses this subject in TCM Service Bulletin M78-8—a highly readable bulletin, the purpose of which (in Continental's words) is "to point out some of the areas commonly overlooked during routine servicing of the ignition system and recommend that efforts be made to determine the cause of the problem(s) rather than immediately changing spark plugs or reducing plug gaps below minimum when occasional ignition system roughness occurs." Continental's maintenance recommendations are, we think, worthy of studious consideration by any operator (of any kind of plane) whose flying regularly takes him (or her) to the upper reaches of the smogosphere. At the risk of repeating some points made earlier (and to be made in chapter 8), we offer those recommendations in digest form here:

1. Always clean *both* ends of a spark plug to like-new condition at every service interval. Don't settle for a half-clean plug.

2. Never accept a plug with chopped ceramic (at either the firing or terminal end).

The Mooney 231 and other lightplanes designed to make themselves at home above 12,000 feet have suffered a high proportion of ignition system problems, due in large part to natural causes.

3. Discard plugs when electrodes have worn to half their original thickness.

4. Set plug gaps at .016-inch (massives *and* fine-wires).

5. Clean all spark plug threads using a wire brush (manual or rotary) with a wire size no greater than .005-inch diameter.

6. After servicing plugs, bomb-test them at 135 psi.

7. Check ignition leads for leakage and resistance using a high-tension lead tester.

8. Check ignition ferrules (terminal connectors) for cleanliness and cracks; clean with lint-free cloth moistened in methylethyl ketone or unleaded gasoline. Do not leave fingerprints on clean ferrules/connectors.

9. Check contact springs for corrosion *and replace as necessary.*

10. Check distributor block and cover plate for signs of carbon tracking or arc-over. Clean all parts thoroughly with unleaded gasoline.

11. Check internal cleanliness of magnetos. Inspect breaker points for signs of pitting/burning; replace if necessary. Check and set point gap (or "E" gap).

12. Make sure magneto-to-engine timing is correct (consult engine nameplate for appropriate limits).

(Copies of Teledyne Continental Service Bulletin M78-8 may be obtained by writing: Teledyne Continental Motors, P.O. Box 90, Mobile, AL 36601, or by contacting your nearest TCM distributor.)

Among other points, these recommendations make clear the close interconnectedness of the elements of ignition systems and certainly the vital place of the magnetos among them. Magnetos demand doctoring, too, of course, and are the subject of this book's final chapter.

Chapter 8

MAGNETOS

Modern aircraft magnetos, with their cams, breaker points, and rotating magnets, may seem relatively primitive next to today's high-output solid-state "point-less" electronic ignitions for cars, but they do have one important design benefit in their favor: They generate their own power, independent of the aircraft's electrical system. Furthermore, they do so quite reliably, without even the need for brushes or commutators.

Nevertheless, magnetos do have shortcomings, which advanced technology can alleviate to some extent but not entirely. As so often is the case with aircraft equipment, magneto troubles are best remedied through steady and skilled inspection and maintenance.

IMPULSE COUPLINGS
AND "SHOWER OF SPARKS"

If magnetos have a major shortcoming—aside from the fact that they contain moving parts—it is that their output varies with rotational speed. This is no problem at the high-rpm end, but at low speeds—such as cranking/starting speeds—magneto output is so low as to be worthless. The "coming in" speed of many aircraft magnetos (the rpm at which a usable spark is produced) is around 200 rpm—well above the cranking capacity of most aircraft starter motors.

And then there is the problem of spark timing. Even if a magneto *could* deliver a powerful spark to the spark plugs at normal cranking speeds, the spark timing of modern aircraft engines (at 20 to 30 degrees before top center of piston travel) is such that—without special provisions for retarding the spark—an engine being turned over by the starter at, say, 90 rpm might well "kick back," producing damage to the starter.

Spring-and-Flyweight Affair

Magneto designers have come up with answers to these problems—special devices that allow aircraft magnetos to deliver an *energetic, late* spark during low-rpm cranking. Perhaps the most famous of these is the impulse coupling, an ingenious spring-and-flyweight affair that bolts onto the rear or drive end of the magneto and causes the magneto to "snap" through its firing position fast—and late (as much as 35 degrees late)—to ensure easy starting. The design of the impulse coupling is such that as soon as the engine has started, the impulse feature disengages (thanks to centrifugal flyweight action), and at all rpm above a few hundred the coupling acts as a drive adapter.

Most (but not all) slick magnetos come with impulse couplings. Quite a few Bendix mags do, too. You can tell if your plane has impulse-equipped mags by hand-turning the propeller in the normal direction of rotation and listening for the loud metallic *snap* of the coupling(s) as you pass top dead center of each compression stroke. If you can hear two snaps, both of your mags have impulse couplings. (Caution: Treat the propeller as though it is "hot," even if you are sure the ignition is off.)

As ingenious and reliable as impulse couplings are, they sometimes give trouble. For instance, the flyweights can become magnetized, locking in the "closed" position so that they do not engage their stop

The magnificent magneto: Generally reliable and good at its job. But to keep it so, you must know your airplane's system, keep the timing in proper adjustment and practice good maintenance.

pins during low-speed cranking. In cold weather, oil can congeal on the flyweight pivots, temporarily immobilizing them in the "off" position—rendering the magneto useless for starting.

Even when impulse couplings are working properly, however, they leave something to be desired in that they produce only one brief spark at the spark plug—which may not be enough to initiate and sustain combustion under severe (cold weather, faulty mixture) starting conditions. Under severe conditions, it would be much more desirable to have a *long-duration* spark at each plug when the piston reaches top dead center on its travel. (But of course, this spark would have to come late enough in the the combustion cycle to preclude engine kick back, as with the impulse-produced spark.)

Creating a Nonstop Stream

The "Shower of Sparks" ignition system, pioneered by Bendix-Scintilla, does just this. It provides a slow-cranking engine with energetic sparks of long duration, late in the combustion cycle, to aid starting; it does everything the impulse coupling is designed to do, only better—and without its drawbacks.

In the Shower of Sparks system a small device called an *induction vibrator* is used in conjunction with an extra set of breaker points inside the magneto—known as the *retard breaker points*—to create a hot, late spark for engine startup. The vibrator—which is an electrical accessory that draws power from the airplane battery—comes on when you engage the starter motor. Its function is to send pulses (around 200 pulses per second) of electricity to the primary winding of the magneto, so that when the magneto's retard points open (very late on the compression stroke), a more-or-less nonstop stream of sparks is created at the spark plug—a "shower of sparks." This sparking lasts as long as the retard points stay open—i.e., through about ten degrees of crankshaft rotation. Contrast this with the single, quick spark that jumps the gap when an impulse coupling "trips." (When an impulse coupling fires, the spark lasts only a few milliseconds—it is extinguished long before the mag's breaker points close.)

The purpose of the retard breaker points in a Shower of Sparks magneto is, as mentioned above, to ensure delivery of a *late* shower of sparks to the cylinders during cranking. The retard points (which are driven, by the way, off the same cam as the mag's normal or "advance" breaker points) are wired through the ignition/starter switch in such a way as to render them inactive any time the starter is not engaged. (Ditto for the induction vibrator.)

BASIC TROUBLESHOOTING AND INSPECTION

In troubleshooting, unless you know what you're doing, there is always a danger that you'll shoot the wrong trouble. This is certainly the case when a mag check on the taxiway indicates that something is wrong—but what? Is a magneto failing? Are the plugs bad? Or is something even worse afoot? It's important to approach the problem from a reasonable perspective.

Reading the Mag Check

Almost every pilot is aware of the fact that the *rpm difference* between left and right magnetos (during pre-takeoff runup) is a more important indicator of possible ignition problems than the actual amount of rpm loss observed for either magneto alone. Most operator's manuals specify 50 rpm as the maximum allowable difference between magnetos during single-mag operation.

The question is, what do you do when—as occasionally happens—the difference between mags during the pre-takeoff runup is noticeably *more* than 50 rpm? (What do you do if, heaven forbid, the spread is more like 125 or 150 rpm?)

There are three possible situations to consider. It could be that [1] you have a normal rpm drop on one mag, but *no* observable drop on the other mag, [2] there is a normal rpm drop on one mag and a larger-than-normal rpm drop on the other mag, coupled with rough engine operation on the "bad" mag, or [3] one mag gives a normal drop and the other produces a larger-than-normal drop, but with smooth engine operation.

If you are seeing no rpm drop on, say, your left magneto—but single-mag operation on the *right* mag produces a *normal* rpm drop—nine times out of ten you can be sure that you have a broken P-lead going to the right mag. (The fact that your left mag isn't giving you an rpm drop would tell you that the right mag is *still firing* even though the ignition switch has been turned from "right" to "left.")

Faulty Ignition Switch?

Taxi back to the ramp and attempt to turn the engine off with the ignition switch only (leave the mixture control where it is). If the engine continues to run, you have a broken P-lead—or a defective ignition switch. Open the cowling and (with the engine off) look at the small wire going from the condenser terminal of each mag to the ignition switch. This is the P-lead for each mag. When the P-lead is broken, the mag is ungrounded and therefore "hot" at all times. (Note: If a rubber sleeve or grommet is covering the magneto/P-lead connection, carefully pry it back. Breaks in this area often go undetected.)

If you are unable to find a broken P-lead, but your engine runs with the switch off and the mixture rich, you undoubtedly have a bad ignition switch. Tip: Have your mechanic check the switch he intends to use as a replacement, *before* he installs it in your plane. There are numerous cases on record—some of them recent—of brand-new ignition switches failing to function correctly, fresh out of the box.

Very important: When performing the "ignition off" engine shutdown check mentioned above, if your engine should indeed stop running, *let it.* Do *not* turn the ignition switch back on when the engine is coughing to a stop or you may encourage a loud backfire, possibly breaking something. Let the engine die, then restart it.

Suppose you have a normal rpm drop (100 rpm, say) on one mag, and practically no drop on the other mag, and everything appears to be working normally (no broken P-leads, no defective ignition switch). Should you proceed to go flying? Probably not. An extremely slight rpm drop (less than, say, 30 rpm) on one mag during your pre-takeoff runup should be taken as an indication of overly advanced timing. Quite possibly, someone has "bumped" the mag-to-engine timing beyond limits in an attempt to correct a large rpm drop on the magneto in question. (This is not an altogether uncommon practice, unfortunately.) Whatever the reason, the mag timing should certainly be checked before further flight, and—if it *is* too far advanced—adjusted per manual specs. Improperly advanced timing has been known to break crankshafts and separate cylinder heads from engines and result in other surprises.

How About the Plugs?

Perhaps a more common (and vexing) problem is that of a large rpm spread between the two mags during runup, coupled with rough operation (stumbling) on the bad mag. (You may have noticed a rough-idling engine during the taxi to the runup area.) One's natural assumption here is that one or two spark plugs have fouled out. How valid an assumption this is depends, of course, on a variety of factors. Is the engine being run on fuel for which it was not designed? (Oil company advertisements notwithstanding, many 80-octane engines do not tolerate 100LL very well. The latter type of fuel has nearly four times the lead content of the former.) Is the idle mixture set too rich? (If you have to lean your engine to get it to idle smoothly, your induction system may be in need of adjustment. In the meantime, expect fuel-fouled plugs.) Is the engine being idled too slowly? (In order for lead to be scavenged efficiently, spark plug core temperatures of 800°F must be maintained—and this is impossible at engine rpm's below 1200.) Have the spark plugs been serviced recently? (If you haven't had them out in the past 25 hours, they may desperately need cleaning.)

If you have a multi-cylinder exhaust analyzer system, you should be able to pinpoint the location of misfiring spark plugs instantly, with the flip of a selector switch, while performing a normal runup and mag check. Finding a misfiring plug *without* the aid of a multi-probe EGT system is almost as easy: Starting with a cold engine, run the engine at low power settings (select the smoothest rpm) for two minutes *on the rough mag*. Then shut it down, open up the cowling, and perform a cold cylinder test (with your hands, if you have to). Obviously, the bad plugs are in the cold cylinder or cylinders—and since you know which magneto gives rough operation, you can quickly trace the ignition wires from the "rough" mag to the trouble-making plug(s) in the cold jug(s). This saves you from having to remove *all* the plugs from the engine for cleaning. The chances are good that any plugs you remove from a cold cylinder (or cylinders) will be thoroughly black in appearance. But before you smile confidently and say to yourself "Ah yes, oil fouling..." (or whatever), stop and ask yourself: Are these plugs not firing because they're *oil-fouled*—or are they oil-fouled *because they're not firing?* After all, if there is a short somewhere between the magneto and the spark plug electrodes, and the plug is not firing inside the cylinder, the plug is going to become fuel-and/or oil-fouled in short order *anyway* by virtue of just being there. Nonfiring plugs get gummed up in a hurry. That's why the manufacturers tell you to keep single-mag operation to 10 seconds or less during runup.

The best you can do is to clean any suspicious plugs very thoroughly *at both ends* (connector-well flashover could be the culprit), check suspicious ignition wires with a high-tension tester, test your cleaned-up plugs(s) in a bomb tester, if your shop will let you do so, and (assuming the plugs check out all right on the test machine) reinstall the plugs in your engine. (For spark plug servicing details, see chapters 6 and 7.)

Moisture or Timing

If the weather has been damp (or you're just washed your engine), you may well find—after pulling and cleaning your spark plugs—that your engine *still* runs rough on one mag, even though you know your plugs and ignition wires are all in good shape. Quite likely, some dew has formed in the wrong place in your magneto(s). The remedy? Gain access to 110-volt A.C., borrow a hair dryer, and give your magnetos a thorough blowing out with warm (not hot) air. In half an hour, you'll be back in business.

When the rpm difference between mags is no more than 200 rpm, and weather (or other) conditions suggest that one mag may have gotten wet, some mechanics recommend flying the engine to bring the mags up to temperature and thereby rid them of moisture. The final decision as to whether it is safe to fly the engine lies, of course, with the pilot. (When *both* mags are wet, this all becomes academic, because you won't be able to get the engine started in the first place.)

Finally, there is the situation in which a normal rpm drop is observed during runup on one mag and a larger-than-normal rpm drop is produced by the other mag, but with normal smooth engine operation the whole time. (No amount of fiddling with the throttle or mixture seems to improve the situation; the rpm drops stay constant.) Here, it is unlikely that a plug is misfiring or firing intermittently (or that a magneto is shorting internally), because the engine *runs smoothly* on either magneto. The problem is likely to be traceable to "timing drift." In all likelihood, the mag with the larger rpm drop has developed late (i.e., retarded) timing. Both mags should be checked before further flight. (Late timing, it its own way, is just as hazardous as advanced timing, since it greatly reduces an engine's power output.)

Contrary to what most pilots have been led to believe, checking magneto-to-engine timing is not at all difficult—nor is it necessarily illegal for pilots to do, so long as *actual timing adjustments* are not attempted.

Basic Magneto Inspection Steps

Many pilots believe that a basic magneto inspection is performed automatically during the annual inspection, that beyond adjusting the timing, the mechanic physically examines the breaker compartment, distributor section, and drive end of each mag. Seldom does that happen.

Rather than relying or hoping that your mechanic will do it—and do it properly—you can perform an on-the-aircraft magneto inspection yourself. In the interest of good preventive maintenance, such an inspection should be performed once a year and discrepancies should be corrected on the spot, rather than waiting for the mags to give trouble before looking inside them—which is the more common (and costly) approach.

Getting under the cowling to give your ignition system a good looking over can save you repair costs, since mechanics seldom inspect it thoroughly, even during annuals.

If you want to stay strictly legal (pilots are generally allowed to *inspect* systems without *adjusting* them, but nonetheless, we're in a regulatory gray area here), have your mechanic undo the screws securing the harness plate and breaker covers to the front of your magnetos—or arrange to be present in the shop the next time these components are off for any reason. The key places to inspect are as follows:

1. Check the distributor block contact springs for corrosion and/or breakage. If unsatisfactory, replace them with new components.

2. Inspect the oil felt washer (it should be wet). If it's dry, add clean 30-weight oil.

3. Inspect the distributor block for cracks or burned spots. The wax coating on the block should not be disturbed; do not use cleaning solvents.

4. Check for excess oil in the breaker compartment. If wetness is evident, it may mean a bad seal or oil seal bushing at the drive end. (Contact a qualified mechanic.)

5. Check for frayed insulation or broken wire strands in the breaker compartment wiring. See that all terminals are secured and the wires are properly positioned.

6. Condensor: Inspect visually. (If possible, test for leakage, capac-

ity, and series resistance.) Note: These condensors are generally reliable for the life of the mag. There's no need to waste money replacing the condensor routinely each time the points are changed.

7. Check the breaker point gap by turning the magneto rotor (i.e., engine crankshaft) until the points are fully open and inserting appropriate feelers. The points should open at least .012-inch, but no more than .024-inch. (If out of limits, have a mechanic adjust the points and recheck the "E" gap. *Any point adjustment will affect the "E" gap.* Therefore, it is best to have a qualified A&P make the necessary adjustments.) Do not attempt to dress the points; replace with new parts if the points are pitted or worn.

8. How about the breaker cam? Is it clean and smooth? (Is the cam screw tight? It should be 25 inch-pounds.) Clean excess grime away by inserting a small strip of high-rag bond typing paper between the cam and follower and rotating the cam through several revolutions. If new points are installed at this time, blot a *small* amount of lightweight oil on the cam.

Note: The next three steps (not applicable to S-200 series Bendix mags) require access to the drive end of the mag and are thus optional for purposes of this on-the-aircraft check.

9. Test the impulse coupling flyweights for excessive axle play by pushing and pulling on the pawls with a bent paper clip. The total in-and-out play should not exceed .016-inch.

10. Check the rotational freedom of the impulse coupling flyweights; excessive friction or sticking may indicate magnetization of pawls. (Bring this to the attention of a mechanic.)

11. Visually inspect the triggering ramp area of the impulse coupling flyweights. A burnished, shiny appearance here means the flyweights are contacting the stop pins while the engine is running—definitely a no-no.

12. Look at the harness. The electrical integrity of the harness is not sacrificed if small areas of the braid show exterior peeling or flaking (the high-temperature coating used on light-weight harnesses is chiefly for vibration protection and chafing resistance); but if more than a few strands of wire braid are broken through, the affected lead(s) may need to be retired soon.

13. Check the springs for corrosion, breaks, or serious deformation. If possible, check the continuity through the lead using a meter or lead tester.

14. Check the insulation plugs (cigarets) for cracks, breaks, or signs of old age. Clean with unleaded gasoline or acetone. Don't touch them with your fingers!

15. Vent plugs: The solid plug should be installed at the top of the mag, while the vented plug should be at the mag's low point. (Owners of S-1200 magnetos: Plug the vent holes with G.E. silicone sealant and drill drain holes in the mag cover as outlined in Bendix Service Bulletin No. 611.)

CHECKING MAGNETO TIMING

Adjustment of magneto timing is a basic maintenance skill, something every A&P mechanic must learn before he or she gets his license. It's a very simple procedure—yet quite critical to engine performance (and engine TBO). Presumably, every A&P knows how to do it.

The mystery, then, is why so many airplanes in the field suffer from improper mag timing. Continental found, some years ago, in an in-house study of incoming engine cores of all kinds, that fully 50 percent of all engines they checked had the timing set well in advance of specs—in many cases, as much as 20 *degrees in advance of the proper setting.*

"These advanced timing settings," Continental concluded, "are believed, in some cases, to be the result of the erroneous practice of 'bumping' magnetos up in timing in order to reduce rpm drop on single ignition."

The problem is particularly serious because [1] most pilots not only don't recognize a shallow (less than 50 rpm) mag drop as a telltale sign of too-far-advanced timing but actually *welcome* such a mag drop—"this baby drops only 25 rpm on each mag...!"—and [2] excessively advanced timing can cause extreme overheating and/or over-stressing of engine "top end" components, leading—quite possibly—to spontaneous engine disassembly.

Make no mistake: Improperly advanced mag timing is bad news for an engine. (It's also more common than most of us have been led to believe.) The only way you can be 100-percent sure that *your* engine isn't improperly timed is, of course, to check the timing yourself—which is something you can do unsupervised, under the preventive maintenance provisions of FAR Part 43, so long as you do not actually make any *adjustments* to your magnetos (or tamper with any wiring).

Timing Set and Drift

Unlike a car's ignition, aircraft spark timing does not change with changing engine conditions: The spark timing in your Cessna or Piper is set once and never varies. The timing must therefore necessarily be chosen in such a way as to favor one engine performance regime; and for an aircraft engine, that means full power, or something close to it. At wide-open throttle and 2,500 rpm or so, the optimum spark timing for most aircraft engines is 25 to 30 degrees B.T.C. (i.e., the spark plugs will fire at 25 to 30 degrees of crankshaft rotation *before* the piston reaches top dead center in its travel on the upstroke of compression). Best power lies closer to 30 degrees B.T.C. than to 25, but the engine manufacturers deliberately put their specs several degrees away from best-power on the retarded side, for two reasons: First, to allow some cushion for uncorrected mag drift; and second, to keep cylinder head temperatures down. "You trade two or three percent of your power— a negligible amount, really—for an extra five or six percent of cylinder cooling," one Continental engineer told *Light Plane Maintenance*. "To me, that's a good trade-off."

Of course, 25 degrees B.T.C. is not the optimum spark advance for an *idling* engine (which is one reason so many aircraft engines idle poorly)—and it is downright unworkable for starting. Special devices—impulse couplings or retard breakers—must be used to *retard* the timing to about zero degrees B.T.C. for cold cranking.

Unfortunately, mag timing, once set, seldom stays put for very long. The problem is wear of moving parts inside the mags. The breaker

The spark timing of airplanes—Cessna, Piper, whatever—is unlike that of automobiles in that it doesn't vary after it is set.

The Eastern Electronics E50 Magneto Synchronizer is just one of many excellent mag timers on the market. All these devices accomplish the same thing: They indicate exactly when the mags' points have begun to open.

points that control spark initiation, for example, can and do erode with time, and the nature of the point-opening mechanism is such that worn points open early, creating too-far-advanced (or "early") timing. Likewise, the cam and follower that trip the points open can also wear with time, and this causes retarded (or "late") timing drift. Both are potentially serious: "Early" drifting mags, left uncorrected, can hasten the onset of detonation and preignition, eventually causing severe cylinder overheating and—very possibly—outright engine failure. (Note also that *one* "early" mag effectively preempts the other mag, on dual-mag operation; i.e., one 30-degree mag plus one 25-degree mag gives you an engine with 30-degree overall ignition timing.) "Late" timing, if left uncorrected, will rob your engine of power and efficiency. These effects are observable on runup. A smooth rpm drop of more than ten percent during single-mag operation (i.e., 175 rpm on a runup at 1,750 rpm) indicates a drift toward late timing. A very small dropoff—less than 50 rpm—means a drift towards early (advanced) timing. Either indication calls for prompt investigation.

Required Equipment

The first thing you'll need to do is avail yourself of a good timing light—preferably a dual timing light like those sold through pilot's supply houses (see any issue of *Trade-A-Plane*). For this article, we settled on the Eastern Electronics Model E-50 Magneto Synchronizer, a lightweight (1.5) pounds), compact (2-1/2- X 3- X 5-inch) battery-operated unit. (There are other fine mag timers on the market, but we chose the E-50 because it has lights *and* buzzers. The buzzer is nice to have when you're working in bright sunlight.)

It's also a good idea to buy or borrow (or make) a piston top-dead-center locator, and a timing-angle indicator. Technically speaking, you don't absolutely *have* to have these items (you can, instead, sight across the timing marks on your crank flange)—but we recommend them. The accuracy of your timing measurement depends, obviously, on the accuracy of these instruments. Alternatively, you can rely on a pencil in the spark plug hole to find top dead center, and the timing marks on your prop flange to determine crank rotation (neither of which we recommend). Or you can make your own TDC-finder and use a protractor and string to determine crankshaft rotation. The latter method is described in detail below.

The Basic Procedure

All timing measurements are made by reference to the number-one cylinder. In broad outline, what you need to do is: [1] Find the number-one cylinder, [2] bring the piston to the top of the compression stroke, [3] turn the crankshaft backwards until the number-one piston is about 25 degrees from reaching T.D.C., and [4] get a precise measurement of the crank's position when the points begin to open in either magneto.

Start, then, by finding cylinder number one and removing its top spark plug. For Continental engines, that means accessing the right-hand (starboard) jug nearest the firewall. For Lycoming engines, it means finding the cylinder corresponding to the *crank throw nearest the propeller*. (It varies from engine to engine.)

Note: For safety's sake, all of the following steps ought to be done only on a cold engine, with *ignition leads temporarily unscrewed from the spark plugs* (to prevent accidental engine firing).

Next, bring the piston in jug number one to the top of its compression stroke. Just put your thumb over the top spark plug hole and turn the prop in its normal direction of rotation until your thumb is blasted off the hole by an outrush of air.

Before going further, it's essential to find—and accurately note—the position of the prop or crankshaft when the No. 1 piston is at top dead center (T.D.C.). Some crankshaft flanges are stamped at the factory with the letters "T/C" and a hash mark to indicate piston-1. T.D.C. when the hash mark is brought in alignment with the crankcase centerline; but owing to parallax viewing errors, this is hardly a foolproof way of finding T.D.C.

The best way to find T.D.C. is to use a top-dead-center locator pin and propeller (or spinner) protractor. The locator is nothing but a solid pin that screws into the spark plug bushing and contacts the top of the piston when the piston is at or near T.D.C. You can make one yourself by machining such a pin, threads and all, at a machine shop, or by taking a worn-out spark plug and welding a U-shaped extension (about 2-1/2 inches long) onto the end. Notice that it doesn't matter how long the pin or "U" is: You're not going to rely on it, alone, to find T.D.C.—rather, you're going to use it *in conjunction with a protractor mounted on the propeller* to find T.D.C. Here's how:

First, screw the T.D.C. locator into the spark plug boss (make it snug enough so it won't shift positions); then clamp or otherwise mount a 360-degree protracotr to the front of your prop or prop dome, with the face of the instrument parallel the prop plane (perpendicular to *terra firma*). Hang a plumb bob on the exact center of the protractor.

Notice that it makes no difference whether the protractor is mounted to the end of a prop blade or the center of the spinner. Wherever you put it, if it's on the prop, it's going to turn with the crankshaft. (You want the plumb line to stand still, and the protractor to turn.)

Also, it doesn't matter what the protractor's initial reading is. (Don't worry about starting out at "zero.")

Now then. *Gently* turn the propeller clockwise until the top of the piston hits the T.D.C. locator pin. (Go slow and don't crunch anything.) *If the piston doesn't hit the pin, you need a longer pin.* After it hits—and you can't turn the prop any farther—make your first note-pad observation: "CW, 250 degrees," or whatever. (If the protractor and plumb line indicate 180 degrees after going clockwise with the prop, write "CW 180." If 35 degrees, make it "CW, 035".)

Next, without changing a thing, turn the prop in *the other direction* until, once again, it will move no farther (i.e., you've contacted the pin with the piston). Obviously, you won't be able to turn the prop 360 degrees—maybe not even 350 degrees—in the other direction, if the piston stopped short of T.D.C. before (which it of course did). So now look at the protractor. If the plumb says 230 degrees, write down: "CC, 230." (Counterclockwise: 230 degrees.)

Suppose your notes say "CW, 250" and "CC, 230." The difference is 20 degrees (that is to say, you turned the prop through a total arc of 340 degrees during the above procedure). *Top dead center therefore lies at 240.* (Split the difference.)

Suppose, on the other hand, your notes say "CW, 035" and "CC, 011." In that case, T.D.C. can be found at the prop position that makes the protractor read 18 degrees (i.e., exactly midway between 35 and 11 degrees on the protractor dial).

Whatever the midway-point is, write it down: 'TDC—240' (or whatever). You've located top dead center.

Point Opening

At this juncture, you're interested in determining exactly where the prop (actually, the crankshaft) is when the points in either magneto begin to open. To do this, you need a hot light—a magneto timer, or mag synchronizer. You also need to spark out your impulse couplings, if present.

The purpose of impulse couplings is to provide a hot, *late* spark for starting. To someone attempting to check mag timing, what this means is that unless special measures are taken to deactivate one or both impulse couplings (some planes have two impulse mags; whereas on some, just the left mag is impulse-coupled), a timing error of up to 35 degrees will be noted. What's more, some timing lights can be damaged by the sudden jolt of high voltage produced when an impulse coupling lets go. To avoid such nastiness, turn your prop in the normal direction until you hear your impulse couplings snap (they produce a loud, metallic *clank* in the normal direction—but no sound in the reverse direction), then back the prop up just far enough to make your timing measurements—i.e., about 30 degrees—but not far enough to reengage the impulse couplings.

Note: If you know for sure that your mags are of the "shower of sparks" type, you needn't heed the previous paragraph. (For more details on identifying and maintaining impulse coupling and shower of sparks, see the following sections.)

Now you're ready to connect your timing light. Start by clipping the black lead wire to a convenient engine ground (such as the hoist ring). Then clip the "left mag" red lead wire to the condenser terminal of

If your E50 Magneto Synchronizer's lights do not come on simultaneously, interpret this as the plugs in each cylinder firing at different times.

your left magneto; and clip the "right mag" lead wire to the corresponding spot on your right mag. (The condenser terminal may be covered by a soft rubber sleeve or grommet. If so, pry it back with a fingernail. But do not disconnect any wires.)

Next, go to the cockpit and turn the ignition key to "both." (This completes the circuit to the magneto primaries. If you fail to do this, both mags will remain ungrounded, and you'll be unable to get a timing reading.)

Once more: Observe appropriate safety precautions. Disconnect the leads from all spark plugs, to prevent accidental engine firing.

Turn your timing light on now and observe the flashing of the lights—or the change in tone of the buzzer—as you slowly move the prop back and forth through an arc of a few degrees. Basically, your mag timer—or mag "synchronizer"—is nothing but an expensive hot light, with two bulbs instead of one (or a buzzer instead of a light). The lights simply come on when the points inside your magnetos open the primary circuit, and go off when the points close (or vice versa, depending on the model of light you're using; the Eastern E-50 lights up when the points *open*).

Do both of your lights come on at the same time? If so, your mags are in synch with each other. If not, it means the spark plugs in each cylinder are firing at diffeent points in the combusion cycle. (For some engines, such as the Continental C-85, this is normal, since the left and right mags are timed two degrees apart.) Notice that in order to check synchronicity, there's no need to locate top dead center or remove the spark plugs, etc.; this is one check you can make literally at any time, on a moment's notice. (Remember that the next time you have two wildly divergent mag drops on runup.)

To check the timing, simply back up about 30 degrees from T.D.C. on No. 1 cylinder, then turn the prop in the normal direction, and keep turning very slowly (the accepted technique is to gently bump the prop tip with one palm) until the timing light comes on, indicating point opening. When that happens, stop, look at the protractor and plumb line (or sight across the timing marks on your crank flange or alternator pulley), and jot down your measurement. Do this for each mag individually, and you're done.

An important *caveat*: Be sure to make your measurement when the points *open* while turning the prop in the *normal direction*. Do not make your measurement while nudging the prop backwards. Gear backlash (of mag drive coupling gears) is considerable—enough to throw your timing results way off if you measure things "in reverse."

Also: If you have a geared engine (GTSIO-520, GO-480, etc.), be sure to take crankshaft gearing into account. Divide prop angles by the crank-to-prop gear ratio to determine the crank angle. For example: 20 degrees of crankshaft rotation on a Continental GTSIO-520 with a gear ratio of 1.5-to-1 produces only 13.3 degrees of prop rotation. Timing measurements are made by reference to crankshaft angles, not prop angles, so this is not a trivial consideration.

You can, as stated earlier, dispense with protractors and T.D.C. locators altogether, if you wish, and rely on the time-honored (but notoriously inaccurate) "sight" method, wherein you simply [1] hook up your timing light, [2] nudge the prop until breaker-point opening occurs, and [3] sight across the timing marks on your crankshaft prop flange or generator pulley (or wherever the timing marks are for your engine). But timing marks are difficult to read, parallax viewing errors of up to five degrees are inevitable, and—in any case—the timing marks may no longer correspond to reality, if the engine has been through one or more field overhauls.

The Polaroid Method

Let's say your engine doesn't have timing marks anywhere (or you can't locate them), and you do not have a timing dial—such as the Eastern E-25—with which to measure degrees of crankshaft rotation. Let's say all you *do* have is a timing light—which tells you when your points are opening—and nothing more. Is there any easy way to determine whether your timing is early or late? There is indeed.

After finding the compression stroke on number-one cylinder, bring the piston all the way up to top dead center. To do this, obviously, you'll need a top dead center locator. We recommend a No. 2 Venus Velvet or any comparable pencil, rod, or dowel.

Place the eraser end of the pencil in the spark plug hole; then, letting the pencil ride up and down on the piston, rotate the propeller back and forth by hand as necessary to find top dead center. (Top dead center, obviously, is that point in the pencil's travel where it starts to go the other way.)

Take the pencil out of your engine after you've found top dead center.

Now go around to the front of the airplane with a camera, sight straight down the prop spinner's centerline, and snap a photograph of the propeller. This is photo 1.

Next, connect your timing light to the engine and (assuming you've already "snapped out" the impulse couplings, if any) back the prop up 30 to 40 degrees, then move the prop forward until your timing light indicates breaker point opening in the left mag. Go around to the front of the plane, sight straight down the spinner centerline, and take a photograph of the prop. This is photo 2.

Finally, repeat the above procedure for the *right* mag. Take a picture and call it photo 3. (Note: You will not need a tripod for taking these photos. The important thing is not how far away from the plane you stand each time, but sighting straight down the engine centerline. As long as you sight straight down the prop's center of rotation each time, your photos will be usable for the purposes of this technique.)

To determine left-mag timing, sit down at home with a protractor and measure the angle difference between the propeller in photo1 and photo 2. To determine right-mag timing, compare photos 1 and 3.

Bring in the Mechanic

We don't recommend that you attempt to make actual timing *adjustments* without the aid of a mechanic. However, we do recommend that you write down all the timing observations made thus far—and compare them with the timing specs stamped on your engine nameplate. The nameplate data may say something like: "L mag—22 B.T.C., plus zero minus 2.' Which, translated, means: "Left mag: 22 degrees before top center; maximum, 22 degrees,—minimum, 20."

Keep a record of your timing checks, and you'll be able to track point and follower-wear trends. And then maybe some day *you'll* be able to tell your *mechanic* when your mags are due for an overhaul or timing adjustment.

IDENTIFYING YOUR MAGNETO SYSTEM

As we've just seen, it's important to know which kind of magneto systems(s)—"shower of sparks" or impulse coupling—your airplane carries. It's just as important to understand that this isn't a consistently cut-and-dried matter.

We know of an owner of an early-model Aztec who fell victim to confusion. In frustration he complained that his owner's manual said nothing about using only the *left* magneto for starting his PA23's engines, despite the fact that retard breakers are present only in the left mag of each powerplant. This seemingly minor operational detail had come to the man's attention only after he had destroyed seven Bendix drives in seven starter motors due to severe engine kickback (caused by the premature sparking of the *non*-retarded right mags) while cranking with both mags hot.

Left or Both?

Most pilots are familiar with the shower of sparks ignition system—a system in which battery power is used to deliver a continuous shower of sparks to the spark plugs, at a late point in the combustion cycle (as determined by a pair of *retard breaker points*). But apparently not all pilots realize that when the shower of sparks system is in place, it is usually incorporated only in an engine's *left* magneto. In such airplanes, it is customary to select only the left mag when cranking the engine—unless, as is often the case in single-engine aircraft (where a key must do the work of several toggle switches), the ignition switch

The Cessna 310 was one of several types that used the Shower of Sparks system during the 1950 and 1960s.

is of a type that cuts out the right mag upon starter engagement. With the latter type of ignition switch, you can safely start any plane on "both." In some older twins, however—and many older singles using a push-button starter—cranking with the mags on "both" can result in severe engine kickback and/or starter damage.

The point is, it pays—literally—to know your aircraft's systems (and follow the handbook-recommended procedures).

If you happen to know that your airplane's mags are of the Bendix -200 series, you can be certain that your ignition is of the shower of sparks type. (This type of magneto was used on many aircraft of the late 1950s and 1960s, ranging from TriPacers to Mooneys to Cherokees and Cessna 310s.) It should be noted, however, that within a given aircraft model series, different mags were often used. Just because the *last* Aztec you flew had retard-breaker mags doesn't necessarily mean that the *next* one you fly can't have impulse-coupled mags. You don't know until you check.

How to Check

How can you find out, simply and quickly, which type of magnetos—shower of sparks or impulse-coupling equipped—a given engine has? Pull the prop through in the normal direction of rotation (observing proper safety precautions—i.e., an observer in the cockpit, the keys in your pocket, and the engine stone cold with the mixture in idle cutoff) and listen. If you can hear a loud metallic clank as you pass top center of each compression stroke, at least one of your magnetos has an impulse coupling. Two clanks, two couplings.

If the above test fails to produce the distinctive metallic snapping of an impulse coupling, you probably have a shower of spark ignition system (or else defective impulse couplings). To confirm the diagnosis, listen for the 200-Hz buzz of an induction vibrator as a properly qualified observer engages the "start" button in the cabin (left mag on—again, exercise caution). You should be able to hear the buzz change in tone as the retard points in the left mag open and close. Alternatively: open the cowl and inspect both mags visually. If one is wired for an induction vibrator and says "Bendix S6LN-201" (or anything else with -200, -201, etc. in the designator) on the nameplate, you've got a shower of sparks system.

INSPECTING MAGNETO IMPULSE COUPLINGS

Impulse couplings (those spring-loaded, centrifugally controlled drive adapters that allow your magnetos to deliver a hot, late spark for starting) seldom require maintenance, but they do wear out, and when they wear out, very bad things happen, not just to the magnetos but to your engine as well.

For example, when flyweight posts fatigue-fail, the coupling's flyweights can drop right down into the accessory case behind your engine, where they can wreak havoc with gearing and oil flow, possibly sending bits of metal throughout the engine oil system. Failed cam stops can do the same thing. Hence, it pays to inspect coupling components periodically.

According to Bendix, "periodically" should mean once every 500 hours. Good practice dictates that the couplings also be checked any time the magnetos are removed from the airplane; but this is not always shop policy.

We have a suggestion: Why not arrange to inspect your magneto impulse couplings yourself, at your next scheduled (or unscheduled) mag-to-engine timing readjustment? The precedure is fairly simple—and it could well end up

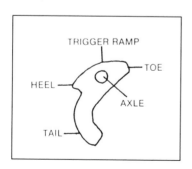

Coupling terminology

saving you a premature engine teardown. (Two years ago, when we made an unscheduled inspection of our Skylane's impulse couplings—mounted on a pair of Slick 662s—we were mortified to find loose coupling pawls. They weren't just loose—they were wobbly. Time in service: unknown.)

Pliers Technique

The usual method of checking the security of impulse coupling pawls or flyweights is to remove the coupling(s) from the mag(s) and inspect the flyweight hold-down rivets, which are only visible from the back (or magneto) side of the coupling.

Slick's pawls are held on by fat, tempered-steel rivets; their security is checked by attempting to rotate the rivets with pliers. (There must be zero movement.)

Bendix machines its cam and flyweight axles from a solid billet of steel; there are no rivets. The flyweights are held on their posts by washers (one per flyweight) which are clinched (hot-riveted) to the studs. Here, the standard inspection procedure is to grab the washers one at a time with light-duty pliers and attempt to rotate them. There should be no movement. (As a matter of fact, though, an A&P/IA of our acquaintance recently told us that he rejects a high percentage of factory-new Bendix couplings due to loose washers. There is some question in his mind—and ours—as to the validity of the pliers test and as to the tightness of the washers as they leave the factory.)

These are the *standard* ways of checking impulse coupling flyweights. But as we said, to do these checks requires that you have access to the "back" side of the impulse coupling—which in turn means uncoupling the coupling from the magneto. And that requires a special tool (a coupling puller) to which most airplane owners don't have access.

Happily, Bendix has worked out a procedure for inspecting impulse-coupling flyweights with the coupling still attached to the magneto. No special tools are needed, beyond a paper clip and a set of feeler gages; and the procedure is quite thorough and reliable (possibly more so than the conventional pliers test).

Stop Pin Clearance

The first step in inspecting your impulse coupling by the Bendix method is to liberate the magneto from its engine mounting. (You do *not* have to detach the mag from the ignition harness.) This is a simple

In the pliers test, the security of impulse coupling flyweights is checked by grabbing each hold-down washer with pliers and attempting to rotate washer (or rivet, if it's a Slick part) with a moderate turning force. Any looseness is cause for rejection.

matter of loosening the two nuts that hold each magneto in its proper timing orientation to the engine. (You may well need an offset 5/8-inch wrench for this.) After loosening the two hold-down nuts, just pull the mag free.

Now you're ready for phase one of the inspection, which is to check stop pin clearance. If your coupling fails this check, there's no point going on with the rest of the inspection, since you'll probably need a whole new cam/flyweight assembly anyway.

Bend the end of a stiff wire (an unraveled paper clip, for instance) into a right angle, with the angled tip no longer than 1/8-inch. Position the coupling so that the heel of one flyweight is as close as possible to a stop pin; then reach behind the flyweight with your paper clip and pull the flyweight as close to the stop pin as you can. According to Bendix Service Bulletin No. 425A, the clearance between the flyweight heel and stop pin must be "a minimum of .017-inch." (Check it with a feeler.) If less than .017-inch clearance exists, this—in Bendix's phraseology—"is cause for immediate rejection of the impulse coupling cam assembly, or possibly the entire impulse coupling."

Your magneto will have either two or four stop pins, total. (The stop pins are what the flyweights grab against at low engine rpm to delay magnet rotation.) You'll need to perform the foregoing clearance check at each stop pin, *for each flyweight*. That's eight checks, total, if you have the maximum of four stop pins and two flyweights.

The above procedure applies to S-20, S-1200, and D-2000 series Bendix magnetos. The -25 series mag (used on many aircraft, including Senecas, Turbo Arrows, and Mooney 231s) is an exception, since its impulse coupling is recessed into the back of the mag, precluding easy paper clip access. Here, what you want to do, rather than try to weasle a paper clip down into the coupling, is apply pressure to the notched area of the flyweight's heel, which is easily reached, using a stiff wire (Bendix recommends a coat hanger)...*Then* insert the feeler as described.

Flyweight Axle Wear

Assuming your coupling passed the foregoing test, you'll next want to check for advanced flyweight/axle wear. (The check for stop pin clearance is primarily a test for wear in the cam-stop area of the coupling body.) This used to be accomplished with the aid of a special Bendix tool, the P/N 11-10041 Flyweight Gage; but as of June 1980, the Flyweight Gage method was obsoleted by the following technique, contained in Bendix Service Bulletin No. 425A:

Begin by rotating the coupling so as to bring the flyweight axles adjacent to the stop pins. (Note that this position differs from the positioning used to check stop pin clearance above.) Make a stop pin clearance measurement—via feelers—first with the flyweight pulled as close to the stop pin as possible (use your paper clip), then with the flyweight pushed back away from the stop pin. The *difference* between your two measurements will give you the total amount of slop or wear in the flyweight axle. This should not exceed .016-inch. (If it's over, reject the flyweight/-cam assembly.)

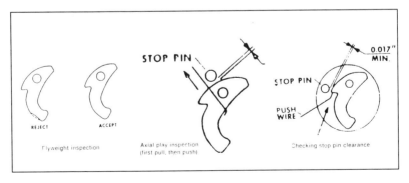

Inspections and Criteria for Coupling Soundness

Tip: Take a look at the trigger ramp area of the flyweight (the outermost edge). If there are any shiny spots along this area, it means the flyweight has been hitting the stop pin(s) while the engine is running at normal speed, as a result of excessive axial wear. Left uncorrected, this condition could develop to a point where the flyweight engages the stop pins at high speed, causing damage. Therefore, *reject the assembly* if it is worn to this extent.

Flyweight Tail Condition

Examine the outer edge of the flyweight tails where they hit the coupling-body projections (the cam stops). The surface at the apex of the beveled edge should blend smoothly with the outer contour of the flyweight. No flattening, denting, or gouging is acceptable. (Remember, if a fatigue fracture gets started in this area, it'll progress to where loose metal gets thrown around in back of your engine—not a pleasant situation to contemplate.)

While you're at it, give those cam stops on the coupling body a good visual once-over; and be ready to reject the unit if you find significant gouging or wear. "Significant" here means that when you drag a fingernail across the surface of the metal, a definite wear step or ridge can be felt.

Also inspect the drive lugs at the drive end of the coupling. Wear steps in excess of .015-inch are considered (by Bendix) cause for rejection.

And don't forget those stop pins. Worn/bent pins should be brought to the attention of an A&P.

Note: The flyweight visual check described above is impossible to accomplish adequately on S-25 magnetos due to the fact that the coupling is recessed well into the mag. A special puller is required to get the coupling off the mag in one piece; check with your mechanic before attempting a detailed inspection of the S-25 impulse coupling.

Magnetization

The coupling body, as mentioned earlier, is made of steel; consequently, magnetization is a potential problem. Due to the design of the impulse coupling, the flyweight tails would tend to stick to the cam-stop ears—preventing the flyweights from engaging the stop pins on start-up—in the event that the body became magnetized. Your engine, in turn, would become well-nigh impossible to start.

To check for magnetization, rotate the impulse coupling (with the axis of rotation always parallel to the ground) and watch to see that the flyweight tails fall free from the cam stops when the tails are elevated. If gravity doesn't cause them to fall free, the tails are sticking—due to magnetization.

Demagnetization involves taking the impulse coupling off the mag, so it's probably best that you leave it to your mechanic to do. There's nothing difficult about the procedure, however. Basically, all you do is place the magnetized coupling over the magnet and shaft of a disassembled magneto, spin the coupling rapidly on the shaft by hand, and invert the assembly, letting the coupling fall into your hand. Do this a few times, and the coupling should become nonmagnetic.

A Word of Caution

Somewhere along the line, you may be tempted to undo the nut atop the magneto drive shaft and pull the impulse coupling off for further scrutiny. Our advice is: *don't.* After removing the nut, if you pull the coupling body away from the magneto, it will separate from the cam assembly, liberating a tightly wound clock spring, and—quite possibly—biting you in the hand. If the spring is damaged, or nicked, it will need to be replaced. What's more, the cam assembly will still be on the shaft; you'll need a puller to get it off, and even then, it may well be stuck in place due to somebody's failure to apply NO-LOK to the shaft before installing the unit originally.

Unless you're prepared to deal with all this, it's best simply to leave the coupling installed on the mag. There's no reason for you to take it off; you needn't remove the coupling in order to accomplish the foregoing inspections (except the pliers test, explained earlier). So leave it be.

Wrapping Up

If your impulse couplings passed the foregoing tests of physical wellbeing, you can loosely bolt the magnetos back in their original positions (approximately), then set the timing, tighten the hold-down nuts, and recheck the final timing just to be sure.

What if, heaven forbid, one or both of your impulse couplings need to be scrapped (due, say, to excessive axial flyweight play)? You go down to your local FBO or mechanic and place an order for a new coupling (or couplings). If you end up ordering new couplings, be double-sure to perform all of the above-mentioned inspections on your replacement parts—don't merely assume that fresh-out-of-the-box components are 100-percent perfect. They often aren't. And whatever the results of your inspection(s), enter them in your aircraft logs. After all, what will your feeler gage measurements mean the *next* time your couplings are checked, if you didn't enter them in your logs *this* time?

TROUBLESHOOTING SHOWER OF SPARKS

Although in many respects the shower of sparks system represents a significant improvement over the impulse-coupling method of starting, the Bendix system does have unique maintenance problems—which can be tricky to troubleshoot, unless you understand the system.

Buzz Vibes

Generally speaking, kick-back during a start attempt signals retard-breaker problems, or a wiring defect involving the retard breaker. (More about this shortly.) If the problem is one of no "kick" at all—back, forward, or otherwise—you could be looking at either a vibrator glich *or* breaker problems. Therefore it is necessary to start by determining whether the problem is or is not with the vibrator. This is easy enough to do: Just listen for the vibrator's 200-Hz buzz while cranking the engine. When you engage the starter, you should hear a loud buzz coming from the vibrator. Furthermore, the buzz should change in tone as the magneto breakers open and close. If you hear no buzz at all, you've isolated the problem. (On some aircraft, the vibrator has its own circuit breaker. Obviously, if you spot a popped "vibrator" circuit breaker in the cockpit, you know your problem is of the vibrator-kaput variety.)

If your battery is low, or if there are any high-resistance (i.e., dirty, corroded) connections in the wiring to the vibrator, the power required to crank your engine may be so great as to leave the induction vibrator starving for electricity when you hit the "start" button. Check the voltage at the IN terminal of your vibrator as someone in the cockpit energizes the starter. (Leave the starter motor connected during this operation; remember, the idea is to see whether the battery is so drained by starter engagement that inadequate voltage is available to the vibrator. Exercise due caution throughout the operation.) The voltage at the vibrator must be at least 8 volts in a 12-volt system—

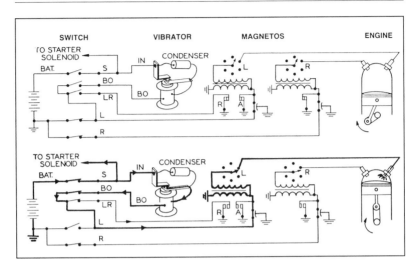

In the typical Shower of Sparks system, the left mag contains retard (R) and advance (A) breaker points, both of which are grounded through the ignition switch when the key is "off" (top diagram). When the starter is engaged (bottom diagram), pulsating battery current is sent from an induction vibrator to the primary winding of the left magneto via the "advance" P-lead. As the piston reaches to-dead-center and the retard breaker opens, the pulsating current creates a "shower of sparks" at the spark plug. [Bendix diagrams]

13 volts, for a 24-volt system—during cranking, in order for the vibrator to work.

Remember that unless you have good, clean connections all through the circuit (and unless the battery is healthy and fully charged), sufficient current may not get to the vibrator, or from the vibrator to the magneto, to create a shower of sparks.

If the tone of the vibrator *doesn't change* as you crank the engine over, check the contact springs in the magneto breaker cover and suspect a short to ground in the P-lead to the *retard* breaker.

If, instead of a changing tone or a constant tone (or total silence), you hear the vibrator *stop* and *start* as the engine is cranked over, the wire to the *advance* breaker is probably broken—or else it has a very poor connection at the mag.

These conditions can be verified by reference to a schematic diagrams showing how the typical shower of sparks system is wired. (Note that on aircraft that use the shower of sparks system, it is customary for only the left magneto to incorporate the retard breaker; the right mag is not used for starting.)

Breaker Problems

Many, if not most, magneto problems can be traced to P-lead and/ or breaker-point problems: burned/pitted points, faulty mag-to-engine timing due to worn points, defective *internal* (E-gap) timing due to worn points, etc. Because a shower of sparks magneto contains *two* sets of breaker points, the opportunity for mechanical mayhem is just about double for these mags—and this can lead to problems with engine starting.

Remember this: If the *retard* breaker doesn't *open*, you'll get no shower of sparks at the spark plugs and no start.

If the retard breaker doesn't *close*, you'll be cranking with a fully *advanced* magneto and a good, strong shower of sparks, a combination that's likely to result in a good, strong kick back.

Retard breaker timing is important. Early breaker opening defeats the whole purpose of having a *retard* breaker. Conversely, late retard-breaker opening can result in the engine firing, but failing to pick up speed and run.

Two sets of breaker points means two P-leads. Look on the front of any shower of sparks magneto and you'll see two wires, two P-leads, going to terminals labeled "switch" and "retard" (or "advance" and "retard"). These wires terminate at the ignition switch.

With any normal magneto having just one set of points, breakage of the P-lead results in a permanently "hot" mag—always "on" because it cannot be grounded through the ignition switch. A shower of sparks mag has two P-leads; again, two chances for mayhem. If, on the one hand, the wire to the *advance* breaker is broken (or has a poor connection at the mag), you'll not only have a permanently "hot" mag— which will show up a zero mag drop on runup—but there will be no way for vibrator current to get into the mag to create a shower of sparks. The tipoff to this condition, again, is the sound of the vibrator: instead of a changing tone, you'll hear the vibrator *stop* and *start* as the retard breaker opens and closes. You'll also witness a failure of the engine to fire.

If the wire to the *retard* breaker should break (or if the connection is bad), you'll get vibrator action—because the vibrator will be grounded through the advance breaker—but retard timing will be lost, and you may get a kick back on starting.

The moral should be obvious: It is a good idea to check magneto connections—both "advance" and "retard"—if not also breaker timing, whenever starting difficulty is experienced. Check the easy things, such as broken P-leads, poor connections, etc., *first.*

Low-Battery Starting Tricks

As mentioned before, a low-battery condition can quickly lead to a no-start situation with this type of ignition system, since some battery power is required to energize the induction vibrator as well as the starter motor, and there may not be enough power to do both.

Fortunately, the vibrator—while it *does* need a certain minimum *voltage* to work (8 volts in a 12-volt system, 13 in a 24-volt system)—does not draw much current when in operation. So if the aircraft battery can be made to rock the engine over compression, you can often succeed in getting the engine to start by connecting a few flashlight cells in series with the IN terminal of the vibrator.

In an emergency situation where the battery is low and a decision has been made to hand-prop the engine, a successful start can usually be made by disconnecting the starter lead (to remove the starter load from the battery) and holding the switch in the "start" position (to energize the vibrator) while someone pulls the prop through. In many cases, the battery will operate the vibrator all right, as long as it doesn't have to turn the starter too. (Caution: Be extremely careful when hand-propping any aircraft engine, and have an experienced pilot at the controls at all times. Tie the aircraft down, if possible. Consider this a last-resort technique.)

Remember that in the shower of sparks system, the induction vibrator is an essential piece of equipment. If your battery is dead, or your vibrator is defective, you will not get a shower of sparks at the spark plugs—and any effort to start the engine will be in vain.

HIGH ALTITUDES
AND PRESSURIZED MAGNETOS

For some operators, misfire at high altitudes can be a persistent problem. A solution does exist, as first described in *LPM* in February 1982:

Question: What do you do when you find that your turbocharged aircraft (which boasts a critical altitude of 15,000 feet) has *magnetos* whose critical altitude is down around 12,000 feet? (You'd like to fly higher, but can't because the ignition Misfire monster rears its ugly head above FL 120.)

Answer: Tap into your turbo deck pressure reference line and run compressor bleed air into your magnetos' timing-hole plugs. (Total cost: about $25 for the necessary clamps, tees, tubes, and fittings.)

This, in a nutshell, is how Mooney, Bendix, and Teledyne Continental have finally decided to attack the high-altitude misfire problem which has plagued Mooney 231(M20K) owners for many months—and Seneca II and Turbo Arrow IV owners for many years (see Continental Service Bulletin M78-8, dated August 25, 1978.) Mooney Aircraft Corporation has available a kit, fully FAA-approved, enabling M20K owners to "tee" into their intake manifolds with a length of 1/4-inch tubing that leads to another tee fitting, with flexible hoses going to each Bendix S6LN-25 magneto.

The mag-pressurization mod, as conjured up by Mooney, is very simple and inexpensive. No magneto modifications are necessary. Instead, the plug at the timing-window hole—atop each mag—is simply replaced with a special screw-in fitting to accept the flexible pressurization line, and the vent plug at the bottom of each mag is replaced with a solid plug. Other than that, no special sealing techniques are used. And in fact, the mags are quite leaky—but the constant flow of compressed air to the mags is more than sufficient to stifle any unwanted crossfiring or arcing in the distributor section at high altitude (as proved by Mooney's test plane, which at press time had accumulated over 100 hours of misfire-free high-altitude flight).

Old Problem, Old Cure

Magneto pressurization is nothing new, of course. Early attempts to develop high-altitude military aircraft led to the quick discovery that, in rarefied air, distributor arcing occurs with greater frequency due to the fact that [1] ionization always occurs more readily in a vacuum than in the presence or air, and [2] at high cruise altitudes, the magnetos contain very-low-density air, while the combustion chambers (in which the spark plugs sit), by contrast, contain high-pressure gases. Given the choice, the electricity developed by the magnetos would rather jump a low-air-pressure gap (in the distributor) than a high-pressure gap (at the spark plug)—and it frequently did, causing severe, unpredictable engine "stumble" at high altitudes. The logical anwer: supercharge the magnetos as well as the engine. And, in fact, this was done on most high-altitude WWII-vintage aircraft.

Bendix's Scintilla division was at the forefront of this technological advance, building pressurized mags not only for WWII bombers but

To help combat high-altitude ignition problems that have plagued their type aircraft, owners of Mooney 231s (M20Ks) have been offered a modification in which the magneto itself is not changed.

for the peacetime B-36 (where the mags were proved to 50,000 feet). In more modern times, Bendix has supplied pressurized D-2000 and -3000 series magnetos for use on the Piper Navajo Chieftain and Navajo C/R. (One of the original uses of a pressurized mag on a general-aviation aircraft was Jack Riley's bleed-air system for the original Rocket, circa 1962. This installation was substantially the same as that now being used for the Mooney.)

In the Navajo, pressurization is brought to the magnetos, via metal tubing, from a deck-pressure pickoff in the induction system. After leaving the induction system, the turbo-compressed air goes through a pressure regulator type valve and (at each magneto) a calibrated overflow orifice. The magnetos are fully sealed; all parting lines are gasketed. This is a much more elaborate (and expensive) system, obviously, than that contemplated for the Mooney 231's Continental TSIO-360-GB engine and S6LN-25 mags. The latter system is unfiltered, unsealed, and unregulated.

Some consideration was given, initially, to the idea of placing an air filter in the Bendix/Mooney "blown mag" system. ("Magnetos are very sensitive to contamination," Bendix's Chuck Shader points out.) But on the basis of tests which showed that the "source" air was, in fact, quite clean, a decision was reached not to incorporate an air filter into the system.

Induction air is, of course, *normally* quite clean. Mooney 231 owners should take note, however, that once the mag-pressurization kit is installed, proper magneto function will depend on regular air filter servicing and proper alternate air door rigging.

Misfire Potential Misjudged

One might well ask at this point, now that the manufacturers have deigned to admit that, yes, the TSIO-360-E/F/G altitude misfire problem is very real and demands a real solution, *why* did it take so long for the manufacturers to come around? (Continental, as mentioned before, acknowledged the existence of a misfire problem back in 1978 when it issued Service Bulletin M78-8; but this bulletin failed to offer any kind of positive solution. It merely called for gapping plugs to .016-inch, and more frequent magneto and harness inspection/servicing. Bendix issued a similar bulletin—Service Bulletin No. 612—in 1980.)

More to the point: How could the certification process allow an airframe or engine manufacturer to certify a 24,000-foot airplane (or engine) with a less-than-24,000-foot magneto?

The answer is that the FAA type certification regulations provide only the *minimum* design and performance standards that must be met by factory prototype aircraft equipped with new engines, new magne-

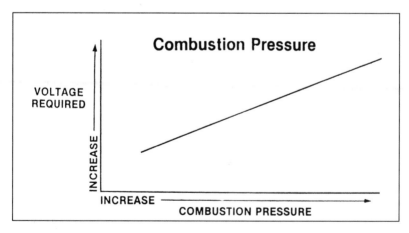

The relationship between combustion pressure and firing voltage is clear: The greater the combustion pressure, the greater the voltage needed to fire the spark plug. Turbocharging keeps cylinder head pressures high; rarefied air makes magneto arcing more likely. Hence the ever-present igh-altitude misfire phenomenon.

tos, new ignition harnesses, new spark plugs, and new turbochargers. *New* aircraft, with new engines and ignition systems, *do* meet their certification requirements, and give "book" performance. It's when things get old (and dirty) that performance degrades—and magneto arcing becomes a problem.

"There's no question about it," says Bendix's Chuck Shader. "A magneto's critical altitude reduces with time in service. Not because there's anything wrong with the magneto, but because spark plugs naturally erode and collect deposits—increasing the voltage needed to fire them—and the mags themselves collect a certain amount of dirt and oil and moisture. All of this increases the likelihood of misfire.

"It's like buying a new car that's advertised to get 30 miles per gallon," says Shader. "Sure, it may get that when it's new. But drive it for 30,000 miles, and you'll find you don't get 30 mpg anymore—for lots of reasons. It's the same way with aircraft ignition systems."

The high-altitude misfire problem is not regarded as a big mystery at Bendix. In fact, Bendix officials are quick to point out that the S6LN-25 magneto used on the M20K was never designed for use at altitudes as high as 24,000 feet (the 231's operational ceiling). But in point of fact, very few magnetos (for general aviation) are.

The bottom line is that Mooney—and Cessna (with the P337) and Piper (with the Turbo Arrow IV and Seneca II/III)—simply misjudged the ability of Bendix -25 series magnetos to perform well at high altitude in normal service.

Mooney admitted the problem and [as of early 1982] took it upon itself to correct it—at no cost to the customer (the mag pressurization kit was provided free to all M20K owners).

The Slick Option

The folks at Slick Electro, in Rockford, Illinois haven't exactly been sitting on their hands throughout the Bendix/Mooney misfiring-mag episode. Slick, in fact, has been hard at work on a pressurized magneto of its own: the model 6224, which is now being installed at the factory on new-production Mooney 231s.

Like the Bendix installation, Slick's 6224 draws high-pressure air from the TSIO-360's induction system at a point near the throttle body. But that's where any similarity between the two magneto installations ends. Unlike Bendix's S6LN-25, the Slick 6224 is fully sealed for pressurization and is rated for 15 psi, versus the 5 to 7 psi developed in the Mooney/Bendix retrofit. (This gives the Slick mag a much higher critical altitude, since one psi equates to about two inches of mercury, or 2,000 feet.) Also, the Slick system uses a paper filter to purify incoming air. "We've found that an air filter is necessary in this kind of system," explains Slick's Tom Lingeman.

Flight testing of the Slick 6224 magneto was carried out in late 1981 in a Mooney 231 modified by Bud Harwood Aviation of Rockford. In 350 hours of test flying, much of it at 24,000 feet, the pressurized mags performed flawlessly. "We are quite happy with the high-altitude performance capability of the magneto," remarks Slick's marketing director, Tom Lingeman. "In fact, we're even seeing some performance benefits at *low* altitudes that we hadn't planned on. For example, the spark plugs run cleaner longer, apparently because pressurization provides a stronger, better-defined spark.

"Also, the magneto itself is cleaner inside. With filtered air flowing through it all the time, you carry off what few contaminants are generated withing the magneto itself. We opened up the flight-test magnetos at about 300 hours, and you should have seen them. They were spotless."

IGNITION MAINTENANCE
FOR HIGH ALTITUDES

Ignition system defects tend to manifiest themselves—as engine roughness—more easily at high cruise altitudes than lower down. It follows that ignition-system maintenance is needed more frequently for high-flying aircraft. According to Teledyne Continental, "It is not uncommon to have to perform complete routine servicing at 100-hour intervals or less when the aircraft is being operated consistently at high altitudes."

When Piper and Teledyne Continental began receiving recurrent reports from the field of engine roughness being observed in Turbo Arrow and Seneca II aircraft during operation at and above 12,000 feet, Teledyne Continental responded by issuing a bulleting (M78-8) containing specific suggestions for inspecting the ignition systems of the affected aircraft. The purpose of the bulletin was "to point out some of the areas commonly overlooked during routine servicing of the ignition system and recommend that efforts be made to determine the cause of the problem(s) rather than immediately changing spark plugs or reducing plug gaps below minimum when occasional ignition system roughness occurs." Although the Continental directive was written in response to problems encountered by operators fo TSIO-360-E and -F engines installed in Piper Arrow and Seneca aircraft, the information is applicable to all engines in all aircraft that regularly operate above 10,000 feet.

Teledyne Continental specifically recommends that the following items be checked on a more-often-than-usual basis in aircraft operated at high altitudes:

Spark Plugs—1. Cleanliness should be equivalent to a new spark plug *at both the firing and terminal barrel ends* after servicing. *The preferred method of cleaning the terminal well is with an abrasive blast cleaner and the proper adapter.* Terminal well cleaning is often overlooked and shows up as "terminal well flashover" at altitude, causing intermittent engine roughness.

2. Ceramic should not be chipped or cracked either in the firing end *or* the terminal well end.

3. Electrodes should not be worn beyond 50 percent of original thickness. Gaps should be set at .016-inch for both fine-wire and massive-electrode plugs (TSIO-360 engines only.)

4. Threads on the shell and shielding barrel should be cleaned with a wire hand brush or power-driven brush with a wire size not to exceed .005-inch diameter.

5. After cleaning and visual inspection, test for satisfactory plug operation using an approved compression chamber test unit. The test pressure should be 135 psi at an electrode gap setting of .016-inch.

Ignition harness—1. Using a high-tension lead tester, check ignition leads for high-voltage leakage and resistance.

2. Check ferrules on spark plug end of harness for cleanliness and cracks. Terminal sleeves should be handled only with clean, dry hands. Clean connectors with lint-free cloth moistened in MEK or *unleaded* gasoline.

3. Check contact springs for corrosion/detonation. *Replace as necessary.*

Distributor block and cover plate—1. Check for signs of carbon tracking or arc-over to surrounding magneto structure.

2. Check grommets for cleanliness and security.

Magneto condition—1. Check internal cleanliness, noting any signs of oil leakage.

2. Check contact point gap and "E" gap (consult appropriate service manual). Always inspect breaker points for signs of severe pitting or

erosion prior to checking point gap or "E" gap; replace as required.

Magneto-to-engine timing—Adjust timing to 20 degrees BTC (TSIO 360-E/F engines only), using the procedures given in section 8 of TCM Overhaul Manual X-30030A. (Timing marks for the LTSIO-360 engine are on the outer edge of the propeller flange at the crankshaft.) The preferred method of engine timing is to use the positive "stop" method of determining TDC in conjunction with prop tip timing disc.

Bottom Lines

The general principles and specific techniques for magneto mainte-nance that we've described should do much to keep your ignition system healthy. Moreover, these principles are well worth following in maintaining all of your airplane's components, if not as a hands-on participant, then as a purchaser of maintenance services and goods. In many ways it pays to:

Know the airplane and its systems, how they function and how they fail.

Approach any service- or parts-purchase decision with care and conservatism; be discount wise and new-price wary.

Be quick to perceive and investigate symptoms of developing problems—poor performance, unusual indications, strange sounds, anything unusual or ominous.

Routinely and unforgivingly inspect your aircraft; don't rely on regulation-mandated inspections or inspectors to serve you with thoroughness.

Heed the regulations' prohibitions regarding owner-maintenance, but take advantage of what you're allowed to do.

Never fly an airplane you suspect is unsafe; don't play for time; remember that machines and devices seldom heal themselves.

In future volumes of the *Light Plane Maintenance Library*, we shall further demonstrate how such principles can be translated into added safety, substantial economies, more comfortable flying, and peace of mind—clearly an agenda worth pursuing.

APPENDICES

Appendix A

ENGINE TROUBLE-SHOOTING GUIDE

Note: The following information is presented for educational purposes only. Before carrying out any of the operations described below, consult FAR Part 43 (which defines who may and may not perform various types of maintenance on U.S. registered aircraft) and appropriate manufacturers' service publications.

High Oil Consumption

POSSIBLE CAUSES	REMEDY	REMARKS
Improper grade of oil.	Change oil; consult operator's manual for recommended type and grade of oil.	Lycoming Service Instruction 1014 offers additional information on choosing engine oils.
Worn cylinder walls and/or piston rings.	Replace rings and/or cylinder as necessary.	If a hissing sound can be heard at the crankcase breather during a differential compression check of the cylinder, excessive ring/liner wear is indicated.
Glazed cylinder walls (failure of new rings to seat properly).	Remove and deglaze cylinder barrels by honing. Replace piston rings.	To aid ring seating, operate newly overhauled engine at high

POSSIBLE CAUSES	REMEDY	REMARKS
		power settings (75% minimum) until cylinder head temperature and oil consumption stabilize (usually within 10 to 50 hours).
Worn valve guides.	Replace guides.	A common problem in air-cooled engines. Prevention consists of using a high grade of oil and keeping it clean.
Excessive oil leaks.	Repair engine as necessary.	To detect leaks, thoroughly wash engine with Stoddard solvent, let dry, then fly for one hour and (afterwards) perform visual inspection.
Clogged air-oil separator (wet-type vacuum pump systems only).	Remove separator from plane and allow to soak in Stoddard solvent.	Check for oil on the underside of plane. If the oil can be traced to the oil separator drain line, clogged separator is throwing oil overboard instead of returning it to the engine.

POSSIBLE CAUSES	REMEDY	REMARKS
Failed or failing bearings.	Replace bearings.	Check for metal in oil screen and/or oil filter before initiating engine disassembly.
Crankcase oil level consistently too high.	Maintain oil at level recommended in airplane owner's manual.	Try operating engine with one quart less oil than you normally allow.
Oil passing through turbocharger seals.	Overhaul turbocharger.	Check to be sure crankcase breather tube is unobstructed. High crankcase back pressure (caused by obstructed tube) will force oil through turbo seals.

High Oil Pressure

POSSIBLE CAUSES	REMEDY	REMARKS
Improper weight of oil.	Change oil.	Use the proper weight of oil for the prevailing temperature conditions as recommended in airplane owner's manual.

POSSIBLE CAUSES	REMEDY	REMARKS
Oil is too cold.	Allow oil temperature to reach normal levels before increasing throttle.	Use engine preheat prior to startup on very cold days (15°F or less).
Oil pressure relief valve not adjusted properly.	Adjust as necessary.	Consut operator's manual for minimum and maximum pressure limits.
Oil passage from relief valve to sump clogged.	Unclog passage.	To detect blockage of passageway, remove pressure relief valve from engine and insert a soft copper wire into oil passage to sump. If blockage is found, remove sump and clean out passageway.
Incorrect pressure relief inside relief valve.	Replace spring with correct part number.	Consult overhaul manual for instructions.
Oil pressure pickup point has been moved on engine.	Relocate pickup point per engine manufacturer's recommendations.	If pickup port position is moved closer to the point of oil pump discharge, higher oil pressure will be observed.

Low Oil Pressure

POSSIBLE CAUSES	REMEDY	REMARKS
High oil temperature.	Check oil temperature gage; look for oil cooling system defects.	Be sure proper weight and grade of oil are being used, and that the oil is maintained well above the minimum safe level. Also check for plugged oil cooler lines; defective Vernitherm valve; inoperative cowl flaps; obstructed oil cooler; incorrect baffling installed, etc.
Insufficient oil.	Keep oil at level specified in airplane owner's manual.	Check to be sure you are using the proper grade of oil.
Inlet side of oil pump is obstructed.	Remove and clean oil suction screen.	Consult engine overhaul manual for instructions.
Pressure relief valve out of adjustment.	Adjust oil pressure to proper limits.	Consult overhaul manual.
Dirt and metal flakes in oil pressure relief valve.	Remove, disassemble, and clean valve.	Check oil screen for signs of metal.

POSSIBLE CAUSES	REMEDY	REMARKS
Damaged oil pressure relief valve seat.	Repair or replace seat as necessary.	Refer to Lycoming Service Instruction No. 1172.
Engine internal damage.	Repair damage.	Check for: worn gearings; crank-case cracks in vicinity of oil gal-leries; loose or missing oil gallery plugs; defective piston cooling squirt passages.
Oil pressure pickup point has moved on engine.	Relocate pressure probe as neces-sary.	Refer to engine overhaul manual.

High Oil Temperature

POSSIBLE CAUSES	REMEDY	REMARKS
Excessive blow-by.	Perform a top overhaul.	Usually the result of worn or stuck rings.
Insufficient cooling air.	Check oil cooler for obstructions to cooling airflow.	Make sure winter baffles are re-moved when flying to a warm region (or when seasons change).
Improper grade of oil.	Use proper grade of oil.	Check aircraft owner's manual

POSSIBLE CAUSES	REMEDY	REMARKS
		for recommended oil grades.
Oil cooler or associated plumbing clogged (or partially clogged).	Remove cooler and/or plumbing; flush with approved solvent.	Refer to engine manual.
Thermostatic bypass valve (Vernitherm) not operating properly.	Replace valve.	Valve base may also need to be replaced if valve has not been seating properly.
Defective temperature gage.	Replace gage.	
Engine running too lean.	Check for induction air leaks; have carburetor or injection system checked.	Observe proper leaning procedures.

High Cylinder Head Temperature

POSSIBLE CAUSES	REMEDY	REMARKS
Engine is running too lean.	Check for induction air leaks; check carburetor (or fuel injector) for proper adjustment; operate engine in accordance with	If this condition is suspect, check spark plugs for gray/white ash-like appearance; also, check combustion chamber for carbon depos-

POSSIBLE CAUSES	REMEDY	REMARKS
	manufacturer's recommendations.	its. An absence of carbon deposits can be considered indicative of lean operation.
Mixture control improperly adjusted.	Check control for proper rigging. Adjust as needed.	Control knob may appear to have full travel in cockpit, yet lack full travel at the carburetor or injection system.
Engine improperly timed.	Check mag to engine timing, adjust per aircraft manual specs.	Inexperienced personnel may have "bumped" mag timing up to reduce rpm drop on runup. If this is the case, your engine will run hotter than normal.
Preignition and/or detonation.	Spark plugs may be wrong type for your engine; try changing plugs. Use only aviation gasoline of the minimum octane rating specified by the engine manufacturer. Lean engine in accor-	Thoroughly examine engine for damage if either of these conditions is suspected.

POSSIBLE CAUSES	REMEDY	REMARKS
	dance with manufacturer's recommendations.	
Cooling baffles improperly installed.	Ensure that all required baffles are installed properly, replace broken baffles.	Never allow existing baffles to be modified or relocated in any way. Consult engine manual.
Plugged fuel nozzles.	Clean nozzles in acetone or MEK; blow out with compressed air.	Consult fuel injection system manual (Bendix, Simmonds, or Teledyne Continental).
Fuel lines of improper part number being used. (Fuel-injected engines only.)	Install proper lines.	Fuel line inside diameter should be .085 to .090". If primer lines have accidentally been installed in place of fuel lines, they can be distinguished by their smaller I.D. (.060", usually).

Engine Surges

POSSIBLE CAUSES	REMEDY	REMARKS
Incorrect prop governor part number.	Replace governor.	Consult engine manual and/or

POSSIBLE CAUSES   REMEDY   REMARKS

POSSIBLE CAUSES	REMEDY	REMARKS
		aircraft parts catalog to verify the correct P/N.
Crankcase breather clogged.	Remove obstructions from breather.	Ice may form in breather in freezing temperatures.
Faulty prop governor.	Replace governor.	
Injector nozzles(s) dirty.	Remove and clean dirty nozzles. Flush in acetone or MEK; blow dry.	This condition may occur following installation of new fuel bladders, which sometimes shed microscopic lint particles into the fuel system.
Air in oil lines or wastegate actuator (turbocharged engines).	Bleed the system.	Continued running of the engine may solve the problem.
Injector nozzle pressure reference system is leaking (turbocharged engines).	Repair as needed.	Check hose connection, O-rings, tubing, etc., for integrity.
Defective oil pump.	Repair or replace pump.	Before replacing oil pump, check to be sure the unit is not sucking air.
Carburetor out of adjustment or defective.	Repair or replace as necessary.	

POSSIBLE CAUSES	REMEDY	REMARKS
Wastegate binding intermittently (turbocharged engines).	Attempt to free the wastegate butterfly with a corrosion penetrant. If this fails, replace defective unit.	To determine if shaft binding is occurring, attempt to move the butterfly through its full travel range with a wrench.
Propeller blades not cycling freely.	Remove prop for overhaul.	A mechanic should check prop blades for proper travel before shipping the unit off to a repair facility for overhaul.

Engine Fails to Develop Full Power

POSSIBLE CAUSES	REMEDY	REMARKS
Low cylinder compression.	Perform a top overhaul.	Confirm diagnosis by means of borescopic examination combined with differential compression test.
Incorrect grade of fuel.	Use fuel of proper octane rating.	
Broken baffles in muffler have blocked exhaust outlet.	Replace muffler.	This is a very common condition, especially with mufflers that

POSSIBLE CAUSES	REMEDY	REMARKS
		have accumulated several hundred hours of service. Engine may operate normally at times as broken baffles move around inside muffler.
Restrictions in air inlet or intake manifold.	Clean/repair system as necessary.	Inspect air filter regularly; replace often. Be sure carburetor heat door is rigged to stay fully closed when carburetor heat is not being used.
Improper fuel flow.	Check fuel system screens for obstructions. Remove obstructions in screens and/or fuel injector nozzles.	Fuel flow gage may also be defective.
Fouled spark plugs.	Clean and test plugs, or replace, as necessary.	
Controllers out of adjustment (turbocharged engines).	Adjust as necessary.	Differential pressure controllers require special equipment for

POSSIBLE CAUSES	REMEDY	REMARKS
		adjustment and may not be adjusted in the field. Other types of controllers can be adjusted in the field.
Throttle lever not rigged properly.	Check for full travel at the carburetor or injector, as well as in the cockpit. Adjust as necessary.	
Damaged turbo impeller; binding turbo wheel(s).	Perform visual inspection for damage and check for free rotation of wheels. Repair or clean as necessary.	Any evidence of damage (e.g., tips of some blades are found missing) will necessitate replacement of turbocharger, since even a slight imbalance in either wheel will cause severe, rapid bearing wear culminating in total turbo failure.
Dirt buildup on compressor wheel (turbocharged engines).	Inspect and clean wheel(s).	Any accumulation of dirt, lead deposits, etc. on turbo wheel will cause an out-of-

POSSIBLE CAUSES	REMEDY	REMARKS
		balance condition leading to rapid bearing wear.
Wastegate out of adjustment (turbocharged engines).	Adjust unit to correct open and closed limits.	Refer to engine manual.
Wastegate stuck in the open position (turbocharged engines).	Remove actuator and loosen wastegate butterfly.	Prevention consists of spraying Mouse Milk penetrating oil on each end of butterfly shaft every 25 hours to preclude corrosion and sticking. (Mouse Milk is approved for use on both Continental and Lycoming engines.)
Oil pressure is too low to close wastegate (turbocharged engines).	See "Low Oil Pressure" chart for corrective actions.	
Wastegate butterfly is warped.	Replace unit.	
Crankshaft to camshaft timing is incorrect.	Remove accessory	Refer to engine manual.

Engine Idles Roughly

POSSIBLE CAUSES	REMEDY	REMARKS
Induction air leak(s).	Fix leak(s).	Check for bad gaskets, induction manifold cracks, poor hose connections, loose flange bolts, etc.
Broken engine mount.	Replace/repair engine mount.	
Mount bushings defective or improperly installed.	Inspect/replace as necessary.	
Uneven cylinder compression.	Rework bad cylinders.	Perform differential compression test on hot engine.
Faulty ignition system.	Check condition of plugs, leads, etc. Replace defective items.	Diagnosis may be confirmed by performing a normal runup and mag check. Rough operation coupled with a large mag drop indicates ignition difficulties.
Primer leaking or not properly locked.	Lock securely; replace if leaking.	
Fuel pressure set too low.	Adjust to minimum pressure limits stated in engine manual.	If pressure cannot be adjusted, replace fuel pump.

POSSIBLE CAUSES	REMEDY	REMARKS
Faulty injector (fuel-injected engines).	Replace unit.	Disconnect induction system at injector inlet to make impact tubes visible. Advance throttle all the way with mixture "full rich," cap the fuel line to the flow divider, and turn on boost pump; if fuel is seen coming out of impact tubes, injector has internal leak and should be replaced.
Plugged nozzles (fuel-injected engines).	Wash nozzles in acetone or MEK, blow dry. Flow check nozzles using vials of identical size to collect fuel; any nozzles that are still plugged will show up easily.	As a further aid to diagnosis, it may be helpful to perform a cold cylinder test.
Idle mixture is set too rich (or lean).	Adjust idle mixture per engine manual.	If engine picks up 150 rpm or more when mixture control is moved to idle cutoff with engine idling, mixture is set too

POSSIBLE CAUSES	REMEDY	REMARKS
		rich. Inspect spark plugs for soot (i.e., carbon fouling) to confirm "rich mixture" diagnosis.
Vapor forming in fuel lines.	Keep ground operations to a minimum; turn booster pump on.	A problem usually encountered on hot days, with a hot engine. While idling, head plane into wind (with cowl flaps open). If possible, line up behind another plane (to catch prop blast).
Sticking valve in fuel flow divider (fuel-injected engines).	Disassemble and clean unit.	Caution: Never interchange fuel flow divider parts. Use care to avoid damaging diaphragm.

High Manifold Pressure at Idle

POSSIBLE CAUSES	REMEDY	REMARKS
Induction air leak.	Repair leak(s).	Engine will probably idle roughly, too.
Incorrect hydraulic lifter P/N installed.	Install correct lifters.	

POSSIBLE CAUSES	REMEDY	REMARKS
Hydraulic lifters bleed down too rapidly.	Replace lifters.	Caution: Do not allow cylinders and plungers to become separated or intermixed during lifter maintenance.
Carburetor or fuel injector improperly adjusted.	Adjust idle mixture to give no more than a 50-rpm increase when mixture control is moved from full rich to idle cutoff.	Idle speed will also have to be set after idle mixture is adjusted.

Split in Manifold Pressure (Twin-Engine)

POSSIBLE CAUSES	REMEDY	REMARKS
Propeller blade angles out of adjustment.	Carefully adjust blades for proper pitch angle at flat pitch stops.	
One air filter obstructed.	Replace obstructed filter.	Problem will be more noticeable when aircraft is at high altitude.
Alternate air door leaking.	Replace/adjust door.	Door may appear to close completely on the ground; however,

POSSIBLE CAUSES	REMEDY	REMARKS
		it may open slightly in flight due to vibration. If this situation is suspected, tape alternate air door shut and fly aircraft to altitude; observe manifold pressure.
Incorrect hydraulic lifter P/N's, or lifters bleeding down too rapidly.	Replace/rework lifters as necessary.	On turbocharged engines, manifold pressure difference may disappear at MP settings above 30".
Controllers out of adjustment (turbocharged engines).	Adjust to proper limits.	With density-controlled engines, some split in MP indications may have to be accepted due to variations in turbo efficiencies.

Engine Will Not Idle Unless Boost Pump Is On

POSSIBLE CAUSES	REMEDY	REMARKS
Engine-driven fuel pump has failed.	Replace pump.	See engine manual.
Engine-driven fuel pump output excessively low	Adjust pump to deliver correct	See engine manual.

POSSIBLE CAUSES	REMEDY	REMARKS
at idle rpm.	fuel pressure.	
Fuel pump bypasses fuel internally (AN-type pumps).	Replace pump.	Refer to engine parts catalog to determine correct P/N.
Fuel vapor bubbles forming in fuel lines.	Operate engine so as to maximize cooling; avoid prolonged ground idling.	
Loose fuel inlet fitting, or a missing (or defective) O-ring, in engine fuel pump (diaphragm-type pumps).	Tighten fitting or replace O-ring as needed. Check O-ring seat for damage; if damaged, replace pump.	Engine may lose fuel pressure as aircraft climbs to altitude.

Appendix B

MANIFOLD PRESSURE GAGE TROUBLE-SHOOTING

SYMPTOM	POSSIBLE CAUSES	REMEDY
High MP at idle.	Air leak in induction system.	Have system checked and—if necessary—repaired.
	Hydraulic lifters are bleeding down too fast.	Lifters should be replaced.
	Incorrect hydraulic lifters installed.	Check part numbers and (if needed) install correct lifters.
	Improperly adjusted carburetor or fuel injector.	Have mechanic check and adjust idle mixture.
MP gage operates sluggishly.	Foreign matter in pressure line.	Have mechanic check line and blow out foreign matter.
	Leak in pressure line.	Have line inspected. See that all connections are properly tight-

SYMPTOM	POSSIBLE CAUSES	REMEDY
		ened; if that does-n't solve the problem (or if line is obviously damaged), replace line.
	Gage mechanism is dirty.	Remove/replace gage.
Gage reads 29" to 30" at all times.	Broken pressure line.	Replace line.
	Faulty mechanism.	Replace instrument.
Excessive needle vibration.	Tight rocker pivot bearings.	Replace instrument.
	Excessive panel vibration.	Inspect and replace panel shock mounts as necessary.
Gage operates in erratic fashion.	Leak in pressure line.	Test line and connections. Repair/replace line. Tighten all connections as needed.
	Faulty mechanism.	Replace instrument.
Excessive gage error with engine stopped.	Condensate or fuel in line.	Have line blown out.
	Leak in pressure line.	(see above)

SYMPTOM	POSSIBLE CAUSES	REMEDY
	Leak in vacuum bellows.	Replace instrument.
	Loose pointer (or pointer has shifted.	Replace instrument.

Appendix C

TROUBLESHOOTING BY EXHAUST GAS TEMPERATURE ANALYSIS

EDITOR'S NOTE: This chart is designed to help aircraft owners with multi-purpose EGT gauges (or "combustion analyzer" systems) identify various specific engine problems that are known to result in aberrant EGT indications. The chart assumes that the reader already understands how the EGT system in his or her plane works and knows what the "correct" termperature indications are for the engine/airframe combination in question, under various operational conditions. The purpose of this chart is to enable the knowledgeable pilot to detect and pinpoint engine "top end" problems *before* the engine gives other evidence. (For more information on EGT systems and combustion analysis, contact Alcor, Inc., P.O. Box 32516, San Antonio, TX 78284.)

SYMPTOM	POSSIBLE CAUSE	REMEDY
Sudden off-scale rise in temperature (for one cylinder, or all cylinders).	Preignition.	Reduce power immediately to bring EGT to normal levels. Land as soon as possible; have borescopic examination of cylinders performed.
75° to 125°F rise for all cylinders.	One magneto inoperative.	Have magnetos checked.

SYMPTOM	POSSIBLE CAUSE	REMEDY
	Improper magneto timing. (Most likely to occur immediately following ignition maintenance.)	Have timing checked and reset.
75° to 125° rise for one cylinder only.	Spark plug not firing.	Return EGT to normal, lower value by enriching mixture. After pinpointing affected cylinder, determine the location of the bad plug by switching between left and right mags. (Mag that produces complete dropoff of EGT indication is the mag firing the bad plug.)
	Induction air leak. (Temperature difference is most apparent during rich-mixture operation.)	Find and fix leak.
Slow decrease in EGT readings for all cylinders with no change in mixture.	Induction ice.	Select alternate air or carburetor heat.
Intermittent drop in EGT for one or two cylinders.	Bad probe or faulty connection.	Replace probe and/or fix bad connection.

SYMPTOM	POSSIBLE CAUSE	REMEDY
	One spark plug is not firing at all and the other is "cutting out."	Check the ignition lead(s) and spark plugs of the cylinder(s) in question.
Lower-then-normal EGT for one cylinder (not intermittent).	Low compression.	Conduct borescopic examination of cylinder.
	Intake valve not opening properly.	Check valve and lifter for proper operation.

Index